CRAFTING MEANINGFUL
WEDDING RITUALS

by the same author

Crafting Secular Ritual
A Practical Guide
Jeltje Gordon-Lennox
Foreword by Isabel Russo
ISBN 978 1 78592 088 2
eISBN 978 1 78450 350 5

Emerging Ritual in Secular Societies
A Transdisciplinary Conversation
Edited by Jeltje Gordon-Lennox
ISBN 978 1 78592 083 7
eISBN 978 1 78450 344 4

of related interest

God, Gender, Sex and Marriage
Mandy Ford
ISBN 978 1 78592 475 0
eISBN 978 1 78450 860 9

Towards Better Disagreement
Religion and Atheism in Dialogue
Paul Hedges
ISBN 978 1 78592 057 8
eISBN 978 1 78450 316 1

CRAFTING
MEANINGFUL
WEDDING
RITUALS

A PRACTICAL GUIDE

Jeltje Gordon-Lennox

Foreword by Tiu de Haan

Jessica Kingsley *Publishers*
London and Philadelphia

Identity icon by © Adaiyaalam CC BY-SA
All other figures and icons © J. Gordon-Lennox
Photos © as indicated

First published in 2019
by Jessica Kingsley Publishers
73 Collier Street
London N1 9BE, UK
and
400 Market Street, Suite 400
Philadelphia, PA 19106, USA

www.jkp.com

Library of Congress Cataloging in Publication Data
A CIP catalog record for this book is available from the Library of Congress

British Library Cataloguing in Publication Data
A CIP catalogue record for this book is available from the British Library

ISBN 978 1 78592 390 6
eISBN 978 1 78450 743 5

Printed and bound in the United States

To couples everywhere who learn
about and from love today and every day.

RITUAL TOOLBOX
LIST OF TOOLS WITH THEIR ICONS

✦	SEVEN DESTRESSING TECHNIQUES
	Remedies (Smell and touch)
	Hugging (Using touch with others)
	Butterfly hug (Using touch alone)
	Near and far (Eyes)
	Humming (Voice and breath)
	Heavenly drum (Ears)
	Finger labyrinth (Touch)

CONTENTS

FOREWORD

There's a magical shop in a cobbled street in North London where they sell vintage dresses. This is no charity shop, with bountiful bargains and colourful bric-a-brac, but rather a museum of antique artworks which happen to be able to be worn on the body.

There are beaded gowns in metallic hues, hung like shimmering paintings on the wall, kimonos of hand-painted silk adorned with muted birds and faded flowers, a rack of improbably dainty shoes. There is a bowl of satin gloves fastened with tiny mother of pearl buttons at the wrist, a glass cabinet displaying buckles and brooches and a vase of ostrich feathers erupting in regal profusion beside the brocade curtain of the changing room.

Imagine a wedding dress is on display. It is clearly made for a woman born in another era, one where we had to contain our emotions, as well as our bodies, in tighter constraints than perhaps we do today. This dress is stiffened with whalebone corsetry, embroidered with intricate patterns, its fragile threads sewn together by a seamstress whose minute, precise stitches show her deftness and skill.

Now imagine asking if you can try it on, watching as it is lowered from its pride of place on the wall behind the till. Imagine drawing back the sweep of the curtain in the changing room, heavy and thick on its brass hoops, pulling off your jeans and boots, wriggling out of your t-shirt, shedding one era in readiness for another. Imagine taking it carefully from its satin hanger and easing it over your head and shoulders, feeding your arms into its delicate sleeves, worried you might snag its lace, inhaling as you slip it over your belly for fear that you might accidentally force its seams as you do so. Perhaps you ask a friend or shop assistant to help do up the innumerable buttons at the back, arranging its flowing fabric to hang over the curve of your hips.

You turn and gaze at yourself in the mirror. You look like you are from another time, transported by the dress into a bride to be who has no mobile phone with which to share her outfit on social media, whose innocence hasn't been sullied and whose romantic ideals haven't been shattered by breakups, broken hearts and pragmatism.

You might quite like this new old you. You might even long for a time of formality and decorum, where you didn't have to feel the weight of so many choices. You certainly love the dress. It's beautiful, after all, so precious and so old, carrying in its folds the invisible echoes of the wedding day of the woman for whom it was made. You can picture her young and blushing as she wore this gorgeous garment, then bright with newness and freshly fitted to her form, now carefully preserved through the years for this moment, unimaginable to its maker and original owner, when a twenty-first-century woman would try it on to see if it might just be her dress. The dress. The one that you will wear on what is purportedly the biggest day of your life.

But it isn't quite you.

It just doesn't quite fit.

It is perhaps a little too small, a little too stiff, the boning of the corsetry a little too tight over a body accustomed to the gym and healthy, hearty nourishment. It comes from an era when we were more willing to confine ourselves into straitened roles, more inclined to hold ourselves back and hold ourselves in. It is beautiful, but it is not us. It is not you.

And, as it is with the dress, so, perhaps, it is with the wedding ceremony itself. The wedding ceremony, with its vows so familiar we may feel inured to the full force of their meaning, its expectations of tradition and formality, its bride being walked up the aisle by a father who is called upon to give away his daughter, to a man who is there waiting to relieve her father of his beloved burden and promise to care for her in his stead… All of these traditions may have their own beauty, their own poetry, their own power and their place – but when put all together, they no longer quite fit.

The stays of the old ways dig into our ribs. They are too tight, too constraining. They afford us a sense of the past, which is valuable and worthy, but they restrict our movement, confine our creativity. They demand that we fit our love into the rules of times gone by, using the expressions of another era, the vows of other men and women. They no longer encompass our expansive world view, our intercultural understanding and our brand new love story, which demands its own telling, its own celebration.

We are too big, too bold, too free and too creative to confine our celebration of the love that is to form the foundation of the rest of our days to the rules of the past. Yes, we can appreciate their beauty and their origin and, yes, we can enjoy their poetry and pageantry, the legacy of the past that brings with it a certain weight, a certain gravitas.

But what if we were free to take the very best of the old and recreate our wedding anew? What if we were liberated to adapt and change the construct of the greatest celebration of love we are likely to experience or at least witness in our lives, and make it our own? And what if we had our very own experienced guide to help us to do just that?

The invitation in Jeltje Gordon-Lennox's book is to bring a new and fresh sense of liberation to this most cherished of rituals. To add in our own emotional needs, our own spiritual beliefs, weaving all the elements together to create a brand new kind of wedding ceremony, one that calls upon the beauty of our ancestry while also allowing us to make it something bespoke and bold, something personal and powerful.

This is a guidebook for wedding ceremonies that can become big enough to encompass our hearts, embrace our complexities and meet our need for independence from dogma. Jeltje is an experienced and versatile guide through these as yet unchartered waters, bringing her creative toolkit to twenty-first-century couples seeking something unique, special and profoundly celebratory.

May each and every wedding ceremony created as a result of this book be suffused with blessings, love and a sense that everything feels like a perfect fit for the unique love story at its centre.

Tiu de Haan
Ritual Designer

ACKNOWLEDGEMENTS

What couple does *not* want a meaningful wedding? The personalized wedding concept is now a mainstream feature of our ultramodern society. Pressure to make the wedding a totally unique experience for wedding guests is extremely high. Unabashedly, the consumer system arouses desire and feeds expectations for a perfect wedding by fabricating glossy hooks that bond couples to the buying process. Borrowing money to cover the often substantial costs of such an event is one thing. Succumbing to the allure of a wedding centred on alien values may well cost a couple their relationship.

First off, I want to express my gratitude to Natalie K. Watson for her enthusiastic support which lead to the publication of three practical guides on creating secular ritual. The team at Jessica Kingsley Publishers admirably rose to the challenge of making accessible this new approach to ritual. After the publication of *Crafting Secular Ritual: A Practical Guide* (2017), which covers six life events or occasions, it was decided that the two main ceremonies in Western societies, weddings and funerals, needed in-depth treatment. This guide deals with wedding ceremonies; *Crafting Meaningful Funeral Rituals: A Practical Guide* will come out later in the year. In particular, I would like to thank team leader Emily Badger, for her ability to keep everyone on track, to production editor Hannah Snetsinger for her good humour and organizational abilities, Helen Kemp for her attention to copy detail, Louise Gill for her skill in clarifying and reproducing my visual world in the layout, Alexandra Holmes for her help with proofreading and publicity executive Lily Bowden for her expert advice. Their patience and close attention to the myriad of details are what turn a manuscript into a book.

My nephew Piet Aukeman deserves credit for wading through an early version of the manuscript. Piet's (im)pertinent questions and suggestions helped me unpack some of my denser ideas. A special thanks to James Peill for stories about life at Goodwood. I am also grateful to Manuel

Tettamanti at the Department of Mental Health and Psychiatry of the Geneva University Hospitals for kindly sharing his research into couple's tensions and conflicts and to Stephen W. Porges and C. Sue Carter for their visionary work on what makes love what it is.

Love and thanks to my children, Sushila and Jefferson, for giving me the physical space I needed to write in our home and for distracting me regularly with silly jokes and photos of their meals and adventures on WhatsApp. I would also like to acknowledge Ian's immeasurable contributions to my life. This year marks 30 years of mutual support in the pursuit of our respective artistic projects.

PREFACE

Congratulations!
Your decision to publicly commit to your partner deserves to be
celebrated in a meaningful way and shared with your nearest and
dearest. I'm honoured that you have chosen me to accompany
you as you craft your unique and meaningful ceremony.

This is how I greet couples who ask me for help in celebrating their union. The ceremony must make sense, first of all to the couple and then to their family members and friends. The practical guide you are holding provides step-by-step support for the creation of an authentic custom ceremony, with or without a professional celebrant.

Few brides wear second-hand wedding gowns, and grooms rarely don fancy dress clearly tailored to someone else's measurements. Yet, when it comes to the ceremony, couples too often settle for off-the-rack or slightly altered wedding rituals. Most are unaware they have a choice. This is particularly the case for fiancés who adhere to no particular religious tradition – sometimes referred to as 'nones'[1] – as well as to those who do not share the same cultural or spiritual practices and of lesbian, gay, bisexual and transgender (LGBT) couples.

The first wedding ceremony I performed was in a religious context for a couple who told me right off that they were not churchgoers; they just wanted something more meaningful than a civil ceremony to mark their big day. The challenge for me, as representative of the institution, was to meet the couple's need for meaning with traditional rites and ancient texts that reflected neither their convictions nor the basis of their relationship. Needless to say, a ceremony that is not terribly relevant

---

1   'Nones' refers to people who do not practise, adhere to or associate themselves with any religious institution.

to the newlyweds is unlikely to have a lasting impact on them or their entourage. This couple's quest for a spirituality that corresponds to the way they live motivated me to consider alternative ways of ritualizing life events. As time went on, I observed that none of the weddings I performed were for couples who attended worship services.

During this same period, I created my first secular ceremony for my sister and her husband. The couple upped the ante by combining it with a naming ceremony for their newborn daughter and honouring their Jewish and Christian cultures. I was flattered by their request and motivated by the challenge. Nonetheless, I saw it as a one-off event: this kind of wedding was for trendy New Yorkers; it was unheard of in Europe where I lived. As we prepared their ceremony, I realized that – trendy or not – this was exactly what the couples who came calling at my Swiss parish really wanted. What should, or could, I do to respond to these couple's needs?

As a representative of a religious institution I was paid to perform traditional rites, even for non-traditional people. As a psychotherapist I am free to meet people where they are at and accompany them as they find their way. As I saw how effective fitting ritual can be for facing and celebrating the uncertainties of life, my frustration with this ethical quandary grew.

All fiancés, whether they are deeply religious, culturally religious or profoundly secular, deserve a wedding ceremony that proclaims to the world who they are as a couple. Ritual accompaniment should be respectful of the culture and spiritual traditions of each individual, couple and family. This conviction lead to a profound shift in my own ritual profile.

Soon after creating the ceremony for my sister and her husband I left my salaried post to craft custom secular rituals for people who need to celebrate their life events, from cradle to grave, with integrity and without the institutional trappings.

Early on, a British couple working in Geneva contacted me to do their wedding ceremony. They explained that, although they would not have minded a church wedding, they did not want to offend religious friends who knew full well that the couple were not practising Christians. Shortly after that, another non-religious couple who practise a kind of Buddhist meditation for two hours every day asked me to help them create their ceremony and include the bride's children from a first marriage. A couple who were engaged on a pier rented a nearby holiday home so that they would have that same view of the lake during their wedding ceremony. A group of buskers who had impressed them on the street a few weeks earlier heralded the bride's arrival in a motorboat driven by her father. Two years later, we crafted a naming ceremony for their daughter.

RESPECT FOR VALUES

As a secular celebrant I was surprised by my clients' enthusiasm for the creation process and their involvement in identifying the profound values they share. I was awed by the power of ritual to enhance their lives and make them feel happier, stronger and more connected to each other.

A couple from Colorado asked me to help them with their wedding ceremony in Paris. This was a second marriage for both of them. As they moved into their late thirties, they observed that their needs had changed. They were less interested in tradition than in a ceremony that authentically marked their mature relationship and commitment. A recent death in the family made it a poor time for a big celebration. So their friends and family organized small receptions for them in four different states. We crafted a ceremony that suited their need for intimacy and adventure in a quiet corner of a public park. After a champagne toast, the photographer and I accompanied the couple to the most famous sites in Paris for their wedding shoot. The newlyweds were applauded at each stop by busloads of tourists and Parisian well-wishers. Years later they wrote to tell me how the words spoken and the gestures accomplished that day supported them in the different trials they faced.

Ritualizing special events, including courtship and partnerships,[2] is an innate behaviour we share with the animal world. A male Adelie penguin living along the Antarctic coast will collect special rocks to attract a female he has his eye on. If the rock he presents her strikes her fancy she will use it to line her nest and allow him to mate with her (Peterson 2016).

---

2   In this context, a partnership is an arrangement between two people, or partners, who agree to cooperate to further their mutual interests by consolidating their relationship. This usually involves a public and exclusive agreement, contract, pledge or vow.

The difference between the Adelie penguin's rock and the engagement ring ritual is that human beings want more from their union rituals than seasonal mating. Human couples expect closeness, meaning and long-term commitment.

In a throwaway society strongly influenced by consumerism, where overconsumption of disposable items is the norm and marriages are notoriously short-lived, couples yearn for rituals they can identify with, that make sense to them and that tend toward long-term commitment. They need union rituals that correspond to their values, that are powerful enough to touch them on their special day and to sustain them as they move together through their daily lives in an unpredictable world.

Working with fiancés on the lookout for 'new rituals' put me wise to a major paradigm shift[3] that untethers ritual from religion. Few of us think of ritual as decorative commodities or sports accessories, but the simple fact that Rituals® global lifestyle brand cosmetics and Ritual® hockey sticks in shiny looks and funky colours have sprung up is proof enough of the unsettled place of ritual in contemporary society. Current dissatisfaction with the ritual status quo is not a rejection of traditional rites but a call to reclaim ritual from institutional – and consumer – monopolies. This paradigm shift is not about replicating the conclusions of tradition – in this case, practising rites that confirm bygone notions of the institution of marriage – but about entering into the same problems as the ancients and making the rituals one's own. That is how a tradition remains alive (Crawford 2015, p.244).

THE PERFECT FIT

An authentic ceremony is the key to a successful marriage or partnership. This audacious statement is not about shiny looks, funky colours and mirroring a global lifestyle. It does not promote a perfect ceremony where everything goes to plan. Authentic means that, like wedding garments, the ceremony should be a perfect fit.

---

3   Scientist Thomas Kuhn popularized the concept of 'paradigm shift' nearly 60 years ago, arguing that scientific advancement is not evolutionary, but a 'series of peaceful interludes punctuated by intellectually violent revolutions'. During these revolutions 'one conceptual world view is replaced by another' (1996 [1962], p.10).

This practical guide is intended as a simple hands-on approach to crafting original rituals for specific situations, people and contexts. It does not tell the couple whether they should marry but helps them express, ritually, who they are together and why they are marrying.

Pertinent questions help the couple concentrate on what is at the heart of their ceremony: What values do we want to convey? How can we transmit them simply and sincerely? What makes sense and feels right to us? Specially designed tools such as *Seven destressing techniques*, the *Questionnaire on my ritual profile* and the *Checklist* keep the fiancés on course while they are creating a ceremony that meets their unique needs.

Those who want a grab-bag of ready-made rituals to celebrate their partnership must look elsewhere. 'Ritual is work, endless work. But, it is among the most important things that we humans do' (Seligman *et al.* 2008, p.182).

Note: This handbook is designed principally for amateur ritualmakers who need to craft a secular ceremony to mark their wedding or partnership. The tools presented here have been forged, tested and tempered with couples and professional wedding celebrants of diverse cultural backgrounds and language groups.

Although it was not originally my intention, I was delighted to learn that the guides can also be of service to institutions in the renewal of traditional religious rites. While I no longer practise formal religion, I admire vital spirituality in all its forms and have great respect for those who dedicate themselves to a specific practice.

This guide may also serve as an aide-mémoire for professional celebrants, but it is not a substitute for celebrant training. If you are searching for a training course, select one that offers personal attention from a skilled instructor, a mentoring system and the stimulation and support of peers. Online instruction is popular now and useful for studying facts. Learning about accompaniment, how to deal with complex situations and preside at real ceremonies, like making love, requires face-to-face interaction.

PRELIMINARIES

Humankind has always felt the need to ritualize. Part I looks at courtship, love and marriage before examining the purpose, function and future of ritualizing unions and partnerships in an ever-changing world. It addresses the role of emotion, the senses, the couple's ritual profile in the ceremonial context of meaningful ritual.

1

THE PROPOSAL

Joe and Amrita shared a chemistry lab table during their last year of high school in New Jersey. Having recently moved to the United States from Montreal, Joe was trying hard to fit in and even harder to impress his pretty and studious lab mate. Amrita had trouble understanding Joe's French-Canadian accent. She remembers him as wild and immature but appreciated his sense of humour.

Ten years later they meet again at a yoga class in New York City and reminisce over smoothies at the club's health bar. They soon become inseparable, and six months later they move in together. Their friends gradually merge in to a close-knit group that spends evenings, weekends and holidays together. Career pressure to accept posts in other cities test the strength of their ties to each other and to their group. Although Joe is tempted to accept work elsewhere, Amrita is reluctant to leave the New York area. She happily talks about their goals for the future but deliberately skirts discussions of marriage. The summer that Amrita and Joe celebrate five years of living together their Swedish friends Filippa and Halvar become parents and three other couples in their group are married.

During a stroll down Fifth Avenue on a crisp Saturday afternoon Joe sees Amrita hesitate in front of a display of engagement rings in a jewellery shop window. Nonchalantly, he asks her which ones she fancies. The following weekend they visit the zoo, spending a long time at their favourite exhibit where they laugh at the monkeys' antics. At one point, Joe catches Amrita's eye and smiles impishly. He assumes the classic down-on-one-knee pose, opens a small box and pops the question. Amrita tears up and simply nods. Joe places the ring on her finger and stands to kiss her. At the sound of applause, Amrita's cheeks and the tips of her ears turn red. Looking around, she catches sight of Filippa and Halvar carrying their baby son Thor. She then recognizes other familiar faces and notices baskets with chilled champagne bottles. A picnic feast follows to celebrate the couple's engagement.

WILL YOU MARRY ME?

The marriage proposal – a ritual in itself! – is an event where one person asks for the other's hand in marriage. If the proposal is accepted, the couple becomes engaged for a variable period which culminates in a public celebration of coupleship,[1] partnership or marriage. In an ideal world, where love and mating are popularly characterized by passion, tenderness and romantic attention, the decision to marry is a choice – the fiancés' choice. The union is loving and lasts until death parts the partners.

Figure 1.1. The proposal
The High Line proved to be the just right setting for this couple. When the young man got down on one knee and presented his girlfriend with an engagement ring, she replied: 'Yes, of course!' – New York City, NY, USA.

© *Victorgrigas CC BY-SA 3.0*

In Western cultures the history of the engagement ring can be reliably traced as far back as ancient Rome. By the twentieth century the diamond

---

1   Coupleship refers to the state of being a couple, being in a committed relationship (Urban Dictionary 2017).

cartel had persuaded couples of the indispensability of the engagement ring ritual. The cartel first educated the consumer about the 4 Cs (cut, carats, colour and clarity) and then promoted the diamond engagement ring as the most sensible for a lifelong relationship. New rings are associated with a relationship that has a clean slate. An heirloom ring may, or may not, be well received. A pawnshop diamond is considered unlucky.

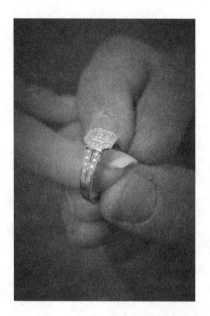

Figure 1.2. A diamond is forever

© Gareth Noble PD [Public Domain]

It has long been assumed that survival took precedence over emotions. Moreover, since human beings produce young that require labour-intensive care over a number of years, scientists also assumed that family or the tribe decided who paired with whom. Romantic love was considered a uniquely modern, if not Western, construction. Recently however, researchers have been examining how human courtship behaviour shapes our species (Carter & Porges 2013; Walker *et al.* 2011). What if emotions are in fact essential to survival?

The stuff of dreams…

HOW TO PREPARE YOUR PROPOSAL

- Clarify what are you proposing: Cohabitation? Partnership? Marriage?
- Choose a setting that has significance for both of you (e.g. in the place where you first met, on a boat, in a movie theatre, at a beach, in a library or a restaurant…)
- Timing is everything! Don't propose before a meal, after a tough discussion, at the end of an evening, when you are tired, anxious, too relaxed or in a foul mood.
- Propose in the classic pose while holding out an engagement ring.

OR

- Use an approach that is typically you: write your proposal in book, on a cake, in a coffee cup, on the sand, on a t-shirt, on a billboard, on a tennis racket or in the clouds… shout it from the rooftops, sing it out opera-style or play it on a guitar.

Above all, *plan, don't improvise!* Keep your proposal simple, the message short – and don't forget to breathe while waiting for the answer.

ROMANCE AND COURTSHIP

Geoffrey Miller argues that the romantic history of our genes goes back to the beginning of humankind. Our minds evolved, not just as survival machines but as courtship machines (Miller 2001, p.3). In the mating market males court and females choose (pp.39, 40, 86, 95). Starry-eyed love is often associated with women, but research reveals that men fall in love faster and more often than women do (Fisher 2016 [1992], p.8).

Hunter-gatherer groups with their relatively horizontal social structures could afford to favour pleasure and free choice.

In urbanized hierarchical systems, where *things* matter, there is more to fight over. People tend to become pawns. Courtship and marriage in this context can have far-reaching consequences on economic, political and kinship interests, particularly on systems such as the British aristocracy. There is an amusing anecdote about how two families, bound together by strong relationships and common concerns, kept that system from collapsing by marrying off their children at a young age.

In 1719 the second Duke of Richmond found himself burdened with heavy gambling debts which he owed to the Earl of Cadogan, who was also an ardent gambler. The duke negotiated the marriage of his first son and heir with the earl's daughter to settle his financial obligation.

When the children first met, Sarah Cadogan was only 13 years old and the Earl of March 18. Although there is little said about Sarah's reaction to the match, the young earl was dismayed at the idea of being wed to 'that dowdy'. The Earl of March was promptly dispatched on the Grand Tour, while Sarah remained with her mother to be schooled on how to be a duchess. After three years of travel and adventure Charles March returned home but seemed in no hurry to claim his bride. His first stop was the theatre where a beautiful young woman surrounded by admirers caught his eye. When he enquired about her identity a bystander informed him that he was looking at 'the Countess of March, the toast of London'.

The two fell profoundly in love. The second duke never tired of entertaining listeners with the story of the young couple's romance.

ALL YOU NEED IS LOVE

Like many modern-day couples, Sue Carter and Stephen Porges met, courted, married and had children. Their career paths are less conventional: Carter[2]

---

2   C. Sue Carter specialized in behavioural neuroendocrinology. She was the first to identify the physiological mechanisms responsible for social monogamy (Winslow *et al.* 1993, pp.545–548; Insel & Carter 1995, pp.12–14). In 2014, Carter was appointed director of The Kinsey Institute and Rudy Professor of Biology at Indiana University. Her goals for the Institute include research on sexual trauma, the transgender movement and medical interventions that can affect a person's sexuality and relationships.

and Porges[3] are internationally recognized experts in their respective scientific fields. Back when emotion was still considered inappropriate as subject of scientific interest they were doing research describing the neurophysiological states that provide the bases for emotional feelings such as empathy and compassion, as well as providing insights into the neural mechanisms underlying love, trust, safety and bonding.

EXPRESSING LOVE

Carter's early research with prairie voles (small rodents) influenced her views of courtship and mating. The urge to mate, considered a biological universal, appears to be based on deep attraction. In mammals this social behaviour is supported by biological components that eventually allow lasting relationships between adults. Moreover, she identified certain molecules[4] that promote love, attachment and bonding among adults and between adults and their young (Carter & Porges 2013). Porges posits that the experience and expression of love among mammals emerges from a neurobehavioural system that promotes closeness, breeding and physical safety (Porges 2011, p.167; 2017, pp.33–51).

Just before Carter became director of the Kinsey Institute, an organization best known for its leading research on sexuality and sexual behaviour, she and Porges collaborated on an article about love for a series on science and sex.

Love is deeply biological. It pervades every aspect of our lives... A 'broken heart' or a failed relationship can have disastrous effects... Without loving relationships, humans fail to flourish, even if all their other basic needs are met... A life without love is not a life fully lived. Although research into mechanisms through which love protects us against stress and disease is in its infancy, this

---

3   Stephen W. Porges is a behavioural neuroscientist best known for developing the polyvagal theory. His theory provides neurobiological explanations for two dimensions of intimacy: courting and the establishment of enduring pair-bonds (1998). It also gives clinicians an organizing principle for the observation of physical and emotional states as well as the treatment of neonates, abused children and traumatized adults.

4   The couple's work examines the influence of two molecules in highly social species: 'the intricate molecular dances of oxytocin and vasopressin fine tune the coexistence of care-taking and protective aggression...oxytocin exposure early in life not only regulates our ability to love and form social bonds, it also has an impact on our health and well-being' (Carter & Porges 2013, p.14).

knowledge will ultimately increase our understanding of the way that our emotions have an impact on health and disease. We have much to learn about love and much to learn from love. (Carter & Porges 2013, pp.12, 15)

During courtship and seduction[5] mammals vocalize, then stop to listen, make eye contact and use other gestures of physical approach and retreat. In doing so the pair limit their vulnerability and the risk of danger or rejection (Porges 2011, pp.167–185). These strategies cost relatively little on the energy scale and allow the partners to engage and disengage quickly if things do not go to plan.

Figure 1.3. Pair of prairie voles
These tiny mammals are known for their monogamous relationships, their faithfulness and mutual affection. According to a recent study, prairie vole couples spend upwards of 50 to 60 per cent of their time together. They calm a stressed partner with the equivalent of prairie vole hugs and kisses (Peterson 2016).

---

5   The courtship and seduction phases take place primarily by communication through encouraging vocalizations (often singing or whistling) and specific facial expressions that include rhythmic bobbing, tilting, swaying, touching, prancing and dancing. While chimps and gorillas hide their sharp canines to expose only their lower teeth, humans tend to smile showing their upper teeth. For both species, eye contact and eyebrow movements also contribute to flirting (Fisher 2016 [1992], p.5).

KEYS TO STEAMY LOVE

Moving on to the sexual engagement phase requires a setting that is perceived as safe for both partners and significantly more physical energy than flirting. Appropriate (non-manipulative) seduction in a secure context, observes Porges, is the necessary condition for intimacy without trauma, particularly for females. Sex for males involves mobilization followed by a period of immobilization where he may feel vulnerable. The female on the other hand is immobile and she needs to experience this immobilization without fear. Suitable courtship and seduction are not just old-fashioned customs but the keys to steamy love. They launch a physical and emotional process that 'changes the visceral and psychological experiences associated with female immobilization from fear to passion' (Porges 2011, p.180).

WHY FORCED SEX IS RAPE

A woman is extremely vulnerable before, during and after sexual intercourse – as well as while bearing and tending children. 'Safety always begins with the body', notes traumatologist Judith Herman. 'If a person does not feel safe in her body, she does not feel safe anywhere' (Herman 2015 [1992], p.269). Not only do her generally smaller size and muscle mass make a woman susceptible to rape by a stranger, but, when her biological need for courtship, seduction and safety are not met she is at real risk to rape by a date – or a husband. The rape of women – but also of children and men – involves immobilization with fear and the inability to defend oneself or flee. This state in turn induces a heightened sense of helplessness that leads to physiological and emotional shutdown. The helplessness and associated shutdown are what make rape the ultimate arm for aggression and torture. Even if the rape victim experiences such a shutdown only once she, or he, may never be able to extinguish the fear pattern, and the deep shame, that comes to be associated with any kind of sexual intimacy.

'Thus, when we are careful about whom we allow ourselves or our children to be physically close to and to have sexual activities with, we are respecting our vulnerability to the conditioning that characterizes passionate love' (Porges 2011, p.180). In short, the process of patient courtship and seduction shows respect for our need to feel safe. It creates an atmosphere of physical intimacy that is basic to the experience of passionate love.

ATTACHMENT AND BONDING

Would it surprise you then that these same conditions facilitate attachment and bonding? And that the absence of feelings of attachment and safety appears to be directly related to mixed feelings about closeness, cohabitation, partnership and marriage? In females, Porges advances, physical immobilization during sexual intercourse without fear heightens their vulnerability to conditioned or learned love. This means that a male who conquers a female's fears by giving her a sense of security and safety is not only allowed to mate with her but can bring her ecstasy. If he earns her trust, in return, she may form a permanent bond with him. By contrast, the male – who is more active during the sexual act – is immobilized and at physical risk from the environment only after ejaculation. Porges conjectures that the male's mobilization may cut him off from conditioned love. Despite that, the male that remains immobilized after copulation, or sleeps with the female, could be just as susceptible as she to learned love (Porges 1998; 2011, pp.167–185).

CONNECTING MIND, HEART AND VISCERA

The proposal ritual marks the end of the courtship phase and the beginning of a whole new chapter in a couple's life that is based on passionate but also learned love. As love evolves it connects the pair at the mind, the heart and the viscera. Gender-specific myths that value chastity and monogamy may well have their origins in this ancient wisdom.

In view of what we have learned about the importance of courtship and seduction, and how feelings of attraction and safety are generated in pair bonding, we begin to see how the Beatles' call for love, love, love may indeed be a timely antidote to growing feelings of isolation, dislocation and fragmentation among individuals but also for society.

So, now that s/he has said: Yes! you may be eager to turn to the next chapter. Don't celebrate just yet. Public commitment can be tough on a relationship. Learn first how to guard against the strain with a few simple destressing techniques (see *Tools: Seven destressing techniques*).

TOOLBOX

★ SEVEN DESTRESSING TECHNIQUES

One day, as I was waiting with the groom, an air-traffic controller, for his bride to enter the garden, he confided that he had just taken Xanax to calm his nerves.[6] Whether you are soon to be engaged or married – or whether you are single and want to be in a relationship – life is often stressful. As a relationship deepens, stability and our sense of safety are put to the test. Strain, and even breakup, can be prevented by timely destressing techniques.

There is no need to resort to dangerous drugs to 'get through it'. We have inherited non-pharmaceutical remedies that can help us destress without any life-threatening side effects. Destressing technology developed by underground mining experts maintains stability and safety by decreasing the risk of rock burst and collapse. As miners drill deeper and deeper into the earth they use destressing techniques that involve softening rock layers, reducing energy storage and releasing rock mass stress.

Learning how to successfully soften rocky times, safely let out excess energy and lower stress levels can make you feel calmer and your life as a couple more secure. It can even influence how you remember the marriage proposal and the wedding. Neurobiological advances open many doors today for understanding and dealing with our 'dis-eases' from a traditional

---

6   Pharmaceuticals should be used with extreme caution. Xanax (generic name: alprazolam) is a powerful benzodiazepine drug used to treat anxiety and panic disorders. Negative effects of the medication may include trouble with cognitive skills, memory and concentration, slurred speech, changes in sex drive and mood, drowsiness, headache. At high doses people may experience, respiratory problems, confusion, disorientation and coma. Overdose on Xanax becomes increasingly likely if used in conjunction with other depressant substances, including alcohol.

body-based perspective. Use these destressing techniques before and during any high stress events that bring you deeper into the relationship.

The seven destressing techniques described below represent corporeal technology that requires no particular conditions or skill. They can be used almost anywhere and anytime by nearly everyone. The nervous groom can do *Near and far* even as he waits for his bride to walk down the aisle. Unlike mind-numbing drugs, these mind–body–viscera-based remedies and exercises use our senses, breath, attention shifts and movement to keep us fully present and in tune with our basic needs and desires.

Remedies (Smell and touch)

Destressing remedies calm the nervous system through smell and touch. One drop of essential oil of rose (*Rosa damascena*), vetiver (*Vetiveria zizanioides*), ylang-ylang (*Cananga odorata*) or sandalwood (*Santalum album*) suffices for rubbing on each wrist and at the base of the neck. Better yet, mix two drops with massage oil and apply to the feet or stomach area. This not only relaxes and lessens stress but reputedly has an aphrodisiac effect. Applied in the same way, lavender (*Lavandula angustifolia*), lemongrass (*Cymbopogon citratus*) and lemon balm (*Melissa officinalis*) combat stress, anxiety and sleeplessness.

Hugging (Using touch with others)

Do this exercise with your partner. It can calm activation, relieve anxiety and feelings of fear. It is suitable for children and adults. Where there is a great difference in size, such as with small children, the person needing soothing can be held. This exercise is not appropriate in the face of real threat. When activation is called for the exercise is counterproductive. Never do this exercise with a person with whom you do not feel very comfortable on a physical level.

- *Positioning:* Stand face to face with your partner with your feet shoulder-width apart and flat on the floor (barefoot or stocking foot is recommended). Place your arms around each other, lean into each other lightly. Focus on yourself. Feel your insides quieting down. Let the hug last until you feel still inside (30 seconds to

3 minutes). An alternative version involves touching foreheads, with or without placing your hands on the other person's shoulders. This version is recommended in contexts where full-length body contact is unacceptable. Rocking has a similar effect and can be done alone (e.g. the rocking in traditional Jewish prayer).

- *For clinicians:* This exercise effectively calms activation. One therapist advises its use to enhance a couple's physical and emotional relationship (Schnarch 1997, pp.157–186).

Butterfly hug (Using touch alone)

The butterfly hug is a self-soothing technique practised alone. It is suitable for anyone who can follow the simple instructions.

- *Positioning:* Turn the palms of your hands towards you and cross your wrists. Interlock your thumbs to form the butterfly's body. Your hands and other fingers are the butterfly wings. Place your thumbs against your upper chest, just below the intersection of the clavicles. (Alternative position: Cross your arms high over your chest and place the tips of your middle fingers lightly on your shoulders, thumbs pointing towards your throat.) Your eyes may be closed, partially closed or even open if you feel safer this way. Turn your eyes inwards towards the tip of your nose.

- *Now you are ready to begin:* Slowly and softly alternate the flapping of your butterfly's wings. Observe your breathing. Bring your breath down into your abdomen. When you feel comfortable with the rhythm of the fluttering, notice any feelings that arise (pleasure, pain, other physical sensations) and what comes up in your mind (thoughts, images, sounds, odours). Observe, but do not judge the feelings or thoughts. Imagine them as fluffy or dark clouds floating high above you. Let a light breeze push them across the sky, beyond your horizon.

- *For clinicians:* The 'butterfly hug' (BH) is a self-administered bilateral stimulation (BLS) method (like the eye movement or tapping) to process traumatic material for an individual or for group work. Desensitization (self-soothing) is a reprocessing by-product using the BH as BLS (Artigas & Jarero 1998).

Near and far (Eyes)

This deceptively simple exercise using the eyes can relieve anxiety and introduce a sense of calm.

- *Positioning:* Place a pencil, a pointer, or use your finger, at arm's length and then draw it towards you until your arm is crooked. Draw your attention and your eyes to the tip of the object or your finger. Now look beyond the tip, along an imaginary line, to the furthest point you can find in the room. Move your eyes back and forth between the points (1–3 minutes). Pause, and then repeat the exercise three times.

- *For clinicians:* This is an exercise I learned from my son. According to David Grand, who calls the exercise 'visual convergence', it activates the oculo-cardiac reflex (OCR), functioning as a primitive, powerful and immediate parasympathetic reflex (vagal manoeuvre), rapidly slowing the heart and calming the body (Grand 2013, p.83).[7]

Humming (Voice and breath)

Humming increases energy, stamina and a sense of wellbeing in a surprisingly short time. Even ten minutes of humming can make you feel regenerated. I learned to bring humming to a new level during Dhrupad (an ancient genre of Indian classical music) workshops with Uma Lacombe (2017). Humming is a marvellous massage of the inner organs!

- *Positioning:* During Uma's workshops we sat in the lotus position, but any upright position is fine, and hummed or sang for 6 to 7 hours a

---

7   David Grand hypothesizes that people with repeated losses or instability at an early age in their relationship with their primary caretakers (attachment issues) feel calmer when looking close (when the pointer [or pen or finger] is nearby) and more distressed when they are asked to look off into the distance (2013, p.87).

day. The beneficent effect is as much due to the voice's stimulation of the body as to the changes that occur with rhythmic breathing.

- *For clinicians:* High frequency sounds of about 2000 Hz and higher are stimulating for the brain. Children's voices and most women's voices are high frequency. Other examples include squeaks, a shrill whistle, flute and the higher registers on a violin. Low frequency sounds tire us more easily because we have to block them out to hear the human voice. Low sounds occur at about 500 Hz and lower; some examples of low sounds include: bass drum, tuba, thunder, deep male voice, machines and traffic noise. Humming and singing activate the vagal nerve and correct respiratory, and thus also cardiac and visceral, rhythms (Tomatis 1988, p.63). Singing and playing a wind or brass instrument can produce a similar effect. Short inhalations followed by longer exhalations 'gates' the influence of the myelinated vagus on the heart (Porges 2011, p.254).

Heavenly drum (Ears)

Have you ever been so tired that you cannot fall asleep? An evening in a noisy environment can produce the same sensation. Taoists teach an exercise that simultaneously rests and stimulates the inner ear; they call it 'beating the heavenly drum' (Chang 1986, pp.128–129).

- *Positioning:* Place the index fingers of each hand on the earflaps that allow you to block out sound. Push lightly on the tips of your index fingers until you cut off outside sounds. With the tip of your second finger, tap gently on the fingernails of your index finger. You should hear a metallic sound, similar to the beating of a drum. Tap a slow and regular but steady rhythm (12–36 times). Do three sets of drumming, pausing briefly between each set.

- *For clinicians:* This exercise stimulates and gives rest to the inner ear. On the one hand, the ear needs a rest from hearing sounds that never cease, even when we are asleep. On the other hand, if the inner ear – what Tomatis calls the brain's dynamo (1988) – is too tired, we often have trouble getting to sleep. In 1954, he introduced the concept of a random sonic event or 'electronic gating system' that 'surprises' the muscles of the inner ear; this revitalizes and allows for a restful state (Tomatis 1988, p.127).

Finger labyrinth (Touch)

A labyrinth is a winding unicursal path leading to a centre. Unlike a maze, the labyrinth does not have traps or blind alleys. Labyrinths are very old. Some date back 4000 years or more. They have long been used symbolically in walking meditation, choreographed dance or as places of ritual and ceremony. The labyrinth evokes metaphor, geometry, pilgrimage. It appears in spiritual practice, environmental art and arenas of social commitment.

Walking through a labyrinth with one's feet, or moving through it with a finger, implies right brain activity. Whenever you feel the need for a break, or the desire to build up your energy or creativity, trace your finger along the white path of this labyrinth to the centre of the circle, pause, then return until you reach the starting point.

Now that you have seen how it works, try alternating your fingers or hands. Synchronizing your breath with the movement of your finger as it moves through the labyrinth can also feel beneficial.

Figure 1.4. Labyrinth

2

WHY MARRY?

After toasting their engagement with friends at a picnic area in the zoo, Amrita pulls a few worn pages from her purse and hands them to Joe. 'Don't Marry'...? Joe looks quizzically at Amrita before smiling at an underscored passage on page 48: "'Don't propose on a wash-day, in the rain, at breakfast or in a tunnel: There is no room for fainting in the former and a narrow chance for time in the latter." I guess the zoo was a good choice then, Amri. You had time and room to faint!'

'What's this all about?' asks newly-wed Kayla as she looks from Amrita to Josh and back again. Amrita explains: 'After my parents' messy divorce and my mother's return to India I vowed never to marry. At the library where I work I found this old pamphlet from 1891 by Hildreth.[1] There are some real gems... Her business model for marriage urges common sense and caution to save society from disgrace – and oneself from misery. I wanted to be rational not emotional about marriage but attending all your weddings these last months has confused me.'

Flipping through to page 27 Kayla says: 'This one is for us, Tyler: "Don't marry a doubly divorced man or woman: It's risky. Something is wrong surely. One divorce should cure any one. Two is a profusion".' 'Sounds like my parents' reaction...' grins Declan as he reads aloud from page 23 to his wife Nelia: "'Don't marry a foreigner: One who comes from a far-away country returns to it. It is very uncertain". What do you think, Nel?'

'Oops, Filippa,' snickers Halvar. 'On pages 31–32 Hildreth says: "Don't marry odd sizes: A tall man with a small woman is awkward enough; but a tall woman with a little, tiny man is a misfit surely. Pair off like soldiers in time of dress parade, with an eye to unity". ...Never mind that we have a kid and aren't married!'

---

1   James W. Donovan used the pen name Hildreth to publish the booklet entitled *Don't marry; or, Advice as to how, when and who to marry* (1891).

Looking over his partner Paul's shoulder Basie interjects: 'Check out pages 35 and 38! Obviously Hildreth wouldn't see our relationship as boosting the serenity of the American system, but I rather agree that no one should marry from pity or for spite.'

Tyler observes dryly: 'It looks like Josh and Aali are the only couple here that Hildreth would approve of. They share the same religion, culture and social milieux.'

'Can't say I'm terribly flattered,' scoffs Aaliyah. 'Check out Hildreth's views on money and beauty: a man shouldn't marry a woman who is rich nor one whose beauty is likely to fade quickly... Josh?!' Joshua chuckles: 'I admit to glancing once or twice at your mother... Listen to her advice to wannabe brides: women shouldn't spurn a man for his poverty, marry for money or accept a proposal from someone too poor (how can one expect her to marry into misery?). Did you consider that, my dear, when you married an artist?'

'How do you all feel about Hildreth's bottom line?' asks Amrita. 'She says we shouldn't expect too much from a man, a woman, or marriage.'

Figure 2.1. You & me together
The couple's relationship is at the heart of the wedding ceremony. The vow and texts are about their joint ritual profile. The ceremony that celebrates their union is a unique showcase of their shared life, values and aspirations.

Figure 2.2. Save the date
Artwork by JGL, based on photo by © Harry Thomas Photography CC BY

Amrita's questions about expectations reflect her ambivalence, not about being with Joe but about marriage. Getting married today often seems like a risky and even unnecessary venture. An internet search for 'why marry?' brings up over 137 million results in less than a second. The top results are about (unmet) expectations. The traditional by-products of marriage such as children, shared responsibilities and property, cooperation with a larger group, increased chances of survival, pleasure and even ecstasy are no longer inseparable from the marital state. In many cultures, unmarried couples can have a perfectly respectable life with or without children. Other factors as unglamorous as politics and economics also influence whether or not people marry. In some countries, like the United States, tax breaks may be an incentive to marry, whereas in others, like Switzerland, married couples pay higher taxes and receive lower social security benefits upon retirement than those who cohabit.

So, why *do* people choose to wed today?

WHY PEOPLE MARRY

The work of ethnologists reveals that marriage as we know it is not universal. Practices around courtship and mating vary enormously from culture to culture, ranging from strict prescriptions in some traditions to no apparent regulation in others. They also evolve, often significantly, over time. In fact, many societies have had a very casual attitude toward what passes for us as marriage. It is pairing up – or 'marriage' as a very broadly defined term – that is thought to be a human universal. As we saw in Chapter 1, fuelled by attraction, seduction and love, we are human courtship machines that move quite naturally towards coupleship.

BEATING ISOLATION

While debate continues as to whether married couples or singles have more satisfying lives, socially connected people do live longer, healthier and happier lives than their socially isolated counterparts (Holt-Lunstad, Smith & Layton 2010). Relationships that are 'medically protective' include marriage,[2] contact with friends and extended family and group membership or affiliation (Sapolsky 2004 [1994, 1998], p.164). Although at least 39 per cent of Americans see marriage as obsolete, a majority of the unmarried say they would like to marry someday (Cohn 2011). The situation of LGBT couples points to the advantages of marriage. Long excluded from

---

2   For simplicity's sake, researchers tend to study the statistics of the officially married and, when compared to the unmarried, married adults tend to live longer and be healthier (Jaffe *et al.* 2007; Johnson et al. 2000). The health benefits of marriage seem greater for men than for women (Troxel & Holt-Lunstad 2013, pp.1190–1192). Married people allegedly have greater life satisfaction, happiness and are at lower risk for depression (Gove, Hughes & Style 1983; Inaba *et al.* 2005). A study of cohabiting and married people in Norway, Germany and Australia shows no self-rated health differences among women (OECD Family Database 2016a).

full participation in civil marriage, this group now has access to public recognition of coupleship, notably legal marriage status,[3] in a number of countries. This change in official status is associated with better health and quality of life among LGBT adults aged 50 and older[4] (Goldsen *et al.* 2017).

REASON AND CHOICE

The advent of urbanization and hierarchical structures reshaped ideals and practices around pairing up and family arrangements. In Western countries, prior to the Victorian era, love was often considered a trivial basis for marriage and a bad reason to marry. As in the case of Charles March and Sarah Cadogan, there were bigger concerns afoot: gaining money and resources, building alliances between families, organizing the division of labor, and producing legitimate male heirs (Wade 2012). The couple expected their parents or guardians to organize their marriage. The family expected to pay for wedding rites and festivities that mirrored their values, religion and social positions. The wedding, often celebrated in spring, served as a fitting coming-of-age rite which solemnized the young couple's sexual relationship and assured them a place in the community. This remains the case today for those who marry very young.

Hildreth's advice was set an era much like our own in that it was financially profitable (at least for some), but unsettled and riddled with crime, poverty and emigration. A few years later, as people emerged from the horrors of the First World War, American playwright Jesse Lynch Williams entertained them with 'Why Marry?', a social comedy that takes a clever humorous look at early twentieth-century society's clashing views of love and marriage.[5]

In the disquieting aftermath of the Second World War, courtship and love came back into the equation with renewed force. Cultural practices around the transition from courtship to coupleship blurred as

---

3   Statistics are for LGBT couples living in the United States.

4   Remarkably, another recent study of married couples shows that many of the acclaimed advantages of marriage disappear when one accounts for early life conditions. The authors conclude that, rather than legislating incentives to marry in adulthood, policy makers would do well to focus on reducing disadvantage in childhood (Perelli-Harris *et al.* 2017).

5   The play won Jesse Lynch Williams the first Pulitzer Prize for Drama (1918).

the decision to marry became ostensibly a choice – the fiancés' choice. Induced by political and religious pressures, the bride promised her groom love, honour and obedience. The latter was often translated by domestic service (cleaning, cooking, childcare and sex) which were recompensed, theoretically at least, by financial support.

FREEDOM AND HAPPINESS

The prosperous 1960s and accessible birth control brought women new freedom. While a wife was no longer legally her husband's property in many countries, her rights and responsibilities continued to be defined differently. She was expected to be loving and hang in there until death parted the partners. In the 1970s, the value of a lasting marriage waned in proportion to the popularity of love relationships characterized by passion, tenderness and freedom.[6]

Figure 2.3. Gender rights demonstration on 8 March 2017 in Paris, France
© *Jeanne Menjoulet CC BY*

6   Divorce rates among American women aged 15 years and over peaked in the late 1970s. then slowly declined until 2000. Although new rises occurred around 2008 and 2011, since then divorce rates have hit a 40-year low (Anderson 2016). Researchers observe that, while marriages still have about a 50 per cent chance of lasting, first marriages are much more likely to survive than second or third. Divorce and marriage rates are influenced by factors such as age at marriage, financial stability and education levels. Those who marry at a later age, are well off and well educated, tend to marry less often and stay together longer (Adams 2016).

Heterosexual and homosexual couples alike, from New York to São Paulo, from Katmandu to Tokyo, now affirm their love relationship is based on gender-neutral roles. Women and men feel free to marry or cohabitate with whomever, whenever and however they want. Most make full use of that freedom to organize the relationship more or less as they please. In exchange for this freedom, both men and women expect – and are expected – to find happiness, sustenance and personal fulfilment in their coupleship.

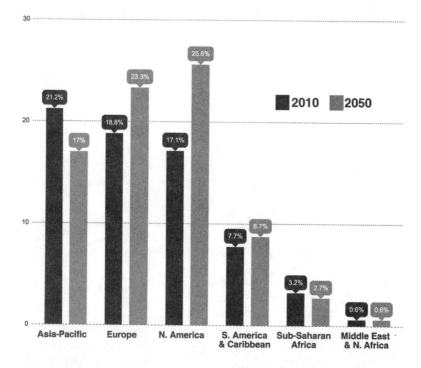

Figure 2.4. Decline in religiosity
The current drop of membership in traditional religious institutions reflects a general trend to eschew religiosity and conventional practices. In 2010 the highest levels of unaffiliated populations were found in Asia (21.2%), Europe (18.8%) and North America (17.1%). By 2050 researchers expect to see the percentage of unaffiliated decrease in Asia (17%) and increase in North America (25.6%), in Europe (23.3%) and in South America and the Caribbean (8.7%).

Data source: Pew Research Centre (2015)

NEW MODELS OF COUPLESHIP

Clearly, our way of pairing up has always influenced and been influenced by social, cultural, religious, political and economic factors. Couples are redefining their values and organizing their lives outside traditional institutions. In Australia, for example, the number of civil weddings increased nearly 75 per cent over religious ceremonies in the last 15 years (Australian Bureau of Statistics 2016). Concretely, this means that couples must find new solutions for celebrating coupleship and other events in their family life. The many different models of coupleship practised today are marked mainly by four phenomena: an increase in women's economic independence and legal equality, the legal gains for unmarried heterosexual and same-sex partners, the move away from religious institutions and their values (see Figure 2.4.), and the rise of new forms and patterns of cohabitation.

FOGGY LENS OF NOSTALGIA

There is a tendency today to decry these changes, and even to blame them for the loss of traditional values. According to historian Stephanie Coontz, this view of tradition comes from looking through a foggy lens of nostalgia at a mostly mythical past. Take the example of licensing marriage by the state or sanctifying it by the church. The practice is more recent than most people imagine. In ancient Rome, the difference between cohabitation and legal marriage depended solely upon the partners' intent. The same condition for marriage was applied by the Catholic Church, which for over a thousand years advocated celibacy over the wedded state. Moreover, two-provider families were the norm throughout most of history and stepfamilies were also more numerous in the past.

There have been several times and places when cohabitation, out-of-wedlock births, or nonmarital sex were more widespread than they are today. Divorce was higher in Malaysia during the 1940s and 1950s than it is today in the United States. Even same-sex marriage, though comparatively rare, has been accepted in some cultures under certain conditions.

... [W]hen it comes to any particular practice or variation on marriage, there is really nothing new under the sun. But when we look at the larger picture, it is clear that the social role and mutual relationship marriage, divorce, and singlehood in the contemporary world is qualitatively different from anything to be found in the past. Almost any separate way of organizing caregiving, childrearing, residential arrangements, sexual interactions, or interpersonal redistribution of resources has been tried by some society at some point in time. But the coexistence in one society of so many alternative ways of doing all of these different things – and the comparative legitimacy accorded to many of them – has never been seen before. (Coontz 2004, p.974)

WHAT DO *YOU* EXPECT?

The new constellation of practices around pairing up and being family is not a problem in itself. The real challenge revolves around expectations. The norm, which used to be a standard pattern of behaviour, is now an awkward bundle of exceptions. In such a context it may take a couple years to work out their gender-neutral roles and to identify common values at the heart of their relationship. In the meantime the pair must also find new solutions for celebrating the different transitions in their coupleship and family life.

 ## NOTES ON REGULATIONS

Marriage may well be an affair of the heart; it is also the only lifecycle transition that is also a legal matter. Marriage laws care not a whit about whether or not you have found your soulmate and they offer no guarantees of happiness. Laws simply regulate who weds and who does not as well as how, when and where people may marry.

Each country, and in some cases each region, applies their own marriage laws. Couples basically have three options: a wedding ceremony that is civil, religious or secular. Variants on these options include unregistered partnerships (Sweden), licensed officiants who may combine the legal aspects of marriage with a religious or secular ceremony (Australia, the United States, Canada and Scotland) and having a religious or secular wedding after the civil ceremony (most European countries).

WARNING

How a country defines marriage has significant implications for your family and financial life, both when you marry and later on. For the most accurate up-to-date information concerning the legalities and requirements, consult the laws of the country, state or territory in which you intend to marry or reside.

AUSTRALIA

Until a popular vote at the end of 2017 brought in marriage equality, Australian law defined marriage as a union between a man and a woman. Cohabitation is the norm in the country (up from 70% to 80% since 2000). When Australians do marry, they increasingly opt for civil rather than religious ceremonies. This was the case for 75 per cent of the couples marrying in 2016 (Australian Bureau of Statistics 2016). Weddings must be performed by authorized marriage celebrants. Information about recognition of unions, including same-sex marriages, contracted in other countries may be obtained from state and territory registries of births, deaths and marriages (Australian Government, Attorney-General's Department 2017).

EUROPEAN UNION

Civil marriage is a legal status recognized in all European Union (EU) countries. Several permit civil unions or registered partnerships as official alternatives to marriage. Couples (including same-sex) who are not registered but live together in a stable and continuous relationship – usually referred to as cohabitation – have some EU-wide rights. In Sweden, for instance, cohabitation is regulated by a special law that applies to two unmarried adults, of the same or different sex, who live permanently together and share the same household. Within the year of the end of cohabitation either party may request the division of property; this is intended as a protective measure for the financially weaker party.

UNITED STATES

The legal requirements and rules around marriage can differ from one state to another. Marriage, civil union, common law unions, domestic partnerships...even the vocabulary may be different. Most terms refer to a marriage-like arrangement but there may be important distinctions. One of the reasons for this has been to allow same-sex couples a way to publicly commit to each other – without quite granting them permission to marry. Some states, such as Vermont, converted all civil unions to marriages after legalizing same-sex marriage. Since 2015, when the US Supreme Court ruled that same-sex marriage bans were unconstitutional, civil unions and domestic partnerships are less relevant.

3

RITUAL POWER

After discussing expectations for marriage the couples' conversation naturally turns to weddings. Aaliyah asks Amrita and Joe about their wedding plans. Joe replies quickly: 'Well, our ceremony won't look like yours. No huppah (traditional canopy), no circling...!' Amrita interrupts her fiancé: 'Why no circling, Joe? In the Hindu tradition, couples circle around a fire seven times...' Joe raises his eyebrows, then turns with relief to Basie and Paul who interrupt to ask about the weddings they missed while volunteering after the hurricane devastation.

Aaliyah and Joshua enthusiastically describe their traditional Jewish wedding and the meaning of the bride's circling the groom. 'One interpretation of this tradition associates it with the ancient battle by Joshua's namesake for the city of Jericho. His army circled it until the walls tumbled down,' explains Aaliyah. 'Leah, our Rabbi, insists that tradition is not static...' 'For us,' Joshua adds, 'the ritual represents the will to break down any barriers between us. Even though it's not traditional for the groom to circle the bride, I did so to symbolize our joint responsibility for honest communication and closeness.'

Declan remarks: 'What I liked best about Josh and Aali's wedding was the music and the dancing!' Nelia demurs: 'Dec, your relatives danced jigs and reels at our wedding.' Turning to the group she adds: 'Declan's family wanted us to have a religious wedding. I just couldn't... So we just had a civil ceremony with a few friends and then a big reception.' Declan adds: 'I envy Filippa and Halvar. They had Thor – without the hassles of getting married!'

'It's different for us,' Filippa explains. 'Here we're the exception; in Sweden we're considered a normal family... I enjoyed all of your weddings, immensely. Each one was so different. I've never attended a wedding like Kayla and Tyler's...'

'We've both been married before,' explains Kayla. 'I'm a pro,' chimes in Tyler. 'This is my third time around! My first – in a church – didn't start

well since I'm an atheist. We both wore cowboy boots for my second...' Kayla confesses: 'My first wedding day felt all wrong, but I didn't have the courage to back out. I vowed then to listen to my gut feelings.' Tyler recounts: 'We checked out different possibilities and interviewed some indie[1] celebrants. Most use a template script and just adapt it, like at the town hall.' Kayla continues: 'We wanted the ceremony to be about us – but we didn't have a clue about where to begin. Tyler is a card-carrying humanist. So, we settled on Terry.' Tyler adds: 'She sussed us out right away. We got some practical tools and the space we needed to create our own ceremony from scratch! It was work, but we learned so much about who we are and how we function together. Unlike my other weddings, this one made me feel married.'

Amrita indicates she'd like Terry's details adding: 'I laughed and cried at your wedding!' Joe picks up on her look and asks: 'What kind of a ceremony will make us feel married, Amri? It seems rather easy to personalize a reception but the ceremony...that's a huge challenge!'

Figure 3.1. Ancient wedding rituals
Indian culture is rich and diverse. Since ancient times bangles are symbols of a woman's married state. While this still holds true today, wearing bangles is now a fashionable trend for the married and unmarried alike.

---

1   Indie refers to 'independent'. In this context an 'indie celebrant' is a person who does not belong to an organization that promotes a particular religion, spiritual tradition or philosophy.

Ritual Power is the new Flower Power.[2] Despite the bewildering images associated with these powers – from Ritual® hockey sticks to psychedelic VW vans – they have captured the collective imagination. Both power movements grew out of the post-war Beat culture that began in the late 1950s and became the hippie movement in the mid-1960s. Both promote love as a means of righting a world that has spun off course. The Flower Power movement, with its accent on peace, sought to raise up humanity from the gruesomeness of war. Ritual Power's emphasis on connection grounds humanity in its earthy *Homo sapiens* roots and serves as a counterpoise to virtual reality, loneliness and a wrenching sense of social dislocation.

Like Flower Power, Ritual Power encourages bodily expression of emotion and appeals to the senses through props like flowers, toys, images, words, incense and music to give form to the feelings of fear, anger and danger inherent in social protest.[3] By facilitating the need for social engagement outside our routine comfort zones these movements represent opportunities to express, separately and together, what it means to be human in our world.

RITUALS ARE POWERFUL PORTALS

Ritual Power is not thought of as something new but rather as an ancient and neutral form of social activity that has been used throughout human history to promote love, healing and social cohesion but also to foment war, hatred and racism. What is new about ritual is the term and our current fixation, and confusion, about this activity.

Fresh discoveries of ancient artefacts, normally of interest only to specialized scholars, now feature in the popular press. NBC News broke the

---

2   The expression Flower Power was coined by the American beat poet Allen Ginsberg in 1965 as a means to transform war protests into peaceful affirmative spectacles (Mandeville-Gamble 2007, p.3).

3   The Flower Power method of guerrilla theatre, which included handing out balloons and flowers with anti-war literature, was epitomized by the Bread and Puppet Theatre in New York City. The ephemeral artistic actions that honour the victims of a disaster or terrorist attack with flowers, toys, candles and notes are examples of the expression of Ritual Power today.

story of a Norwegian archaeologist's discovery of signs of ancient rituals practised some 70,000 years ago in the remote area of Botswana's Kalahari Desert (Britt 2006). More recently *The Washington Post* announced the deciphering of a 1,300-year-old ritual practitioner's *Handbook of Ritual Power* that describes medieval love spells and exorcisms (Jarus 2014). Remarkably, both articles gave the finds a decidedly ritual, rather than cultural or historical, take.

In spite of a growing sense that 'ritual' represents a panhuman phenomenon and that in 'ritualizing' we participate in something universal, like our concept of 'marriage' (see Chapter 2), ritual is a relatively recent, rather abstract idea introduced by scholars.[4] Definitions proliferate;[5] adding yet another one to the pack would be counterproductive. The late nineteenth-century French poet Stéphane Mallarmé seemed to understand this when he said: 'To define is to kill. To suggest is to create.'

SURVIVAL, COMFORT AND COOPERATION

What the term 'ritual' suggests today is our need to 'do something' when faced with change and uncertainty. Throughout human history, societies all over the world developed nodes of culture that we now call ceremonies or rituals.[6] These social activities have always been powerful portals in times of uncertainty, change and transition.

Much has been written about rites and their function in society, points out ethologist Ellen Dissanayake, but one looks in vain in such studies for 'an ultimate function for ceremonial behaviour in a biological or adaptive sense' (2009, p.541). As Dissanayake watched people go about their everyday lives, she noticed that humans everywhere avidly engage in

---

4   Talal Asad suggests that changes in institutional structures and in organizations of the self make possible, for better or worse, the concept of ritual as a universal category (1993, pp.55–80).

5   Ronald L. Grimes presents several pages of erudite definitions of ritual in the Appendices to his book *The Craft of Ritual Studies* (2014).

6   The work of neuroscientists such as Robert C. Scaer (2017, pp.63–67) and Stephen W. Porges shows that human beings are hardwired to ritualize. Porges's 'polyvagal theory legitimates the study of age-old collective and religious practices such as communal chanting, various breathing technics, and other methods that shifts in autonomic state' (van der Kolk 2011, p.xvi).

playful, artistic and ritual pursuits. 'The impetus to mark as "special" an expression or artefact, even our bodies, is deep-seated and widespread' (1992, p.60). She became convinced that these pursuits represent a biologically endowed need that points to a broader category of 'universally observable transformative activity' that she calls artification[7] (Dissanayake 2017, p.161) and identified two ultimate adaptive functions of these activities.

First of all, artification is something to do to allay fear and receive comfort when beset by uncertain circumstances.

> Early humans found attention-grabbing visual, aural, and gestural artifications to be essential in creating and sustaining their emotional investment, as individuals and as a group, in obtaining the life needs they had evolved to care about. This was not a conscious choice. Rather, over time, a cultural group that performed artified ritual practices, thus providing the release of prosocial neurohormones, would become more unified and cooperative and its individuals less anxious compared with groups without artification – with artifiers, over evolutionary time, gradually achieving greater individual and group survival. (Dissanayake 2017, pp.159–160)

The second ultimate adaptive function involves group cooperation and unity. Participation in ceremonies instils collective emotions such as trust and belongingness and coordinates members of the group on the physical, neurological and emotional levels (Dissanayake 2017 [2014], p.25).[8]

'TRADITIONAL' RITES

Wedding rites showcase the couple. Most couples today see their commitment as a strictly personal affair. Yet marriage has significant

---

7   'Artification', a rather awkward term, is apparently more acceptable to scientists than 'making special' or 'doing something'.

8   Affinitive behaviours and emotions, such as those created and reinforced in mother–infant interaction and in arts-suffused ceremonial participation activate the orbitofrontal cortex and other reward centres of the brain. Oxytocin and opioids are released at parturition and during maternal behaviour in all mammals as well as when dancing, listening to music and performing other movement activities in which people participate with one or more others. Oxytocin in particular contributes to instilling trust and attachment and it relieves individual anxiety (Dissanayake 2017 [2014], p.25).

legal and social ramifications. A traditional wedding, whether religious, cultural or civic, publicly proclaims the couple's adherence to institutional values and rites.

In Chapter 2 we looked at how a mostly mythical past, with its supposed loss of tradition, can affect our ideas of what was and is, as well as our expectations of what should be. Likewise, what we now call 'traditional' rites are procedures, gestures and words that were invented by institutions for their members. Adherents who participate in the rites of a tradition they practise often find it a very powerful experience. Practising these rites reinforces the identity, way of thinking and cultural heritage of people who speak the same language and share the same history, culture and values.

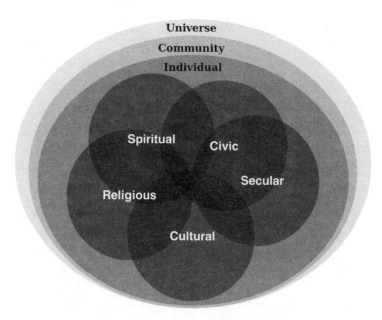

Figure 3.2. Ritual type and scope
Life event rituals are influenced by individual preferences but also by the couple's community and global trends. Formal and informal life event ceremonies can be classified into at least five types: cultural, civic, spiritual, religious and secular. While a ceremony that celebrates coupleship, for example, can have cultural, civic, spiritual, religious and secular dimensions, it cannot be both religious and secular.

RELIGIOUS WEDDING RITES

When people talk of 'traditional wedding rituals' they usually mean religious rites, which are in fact only one kind of wedding rite. Traditional wedding rites can also be civic,[9] cultural, spiritual and secular (see Figure 3.2). Institutional rites require little or no preparation. In some cases, fiancés must follow premarital classes where they learn about the meaning and expectations of marriage in that tradition.

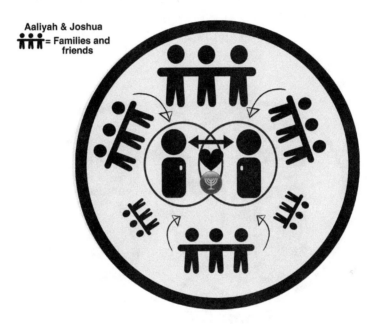

Figure 3.3. Religious wedding rites
Aaliyah and Joshua are shown in this figure surrounded by a supportive circle of people composed of parents, family members and friends. The menorah represents both the central place of Jewish practice in the newlyweds' relationship and their ties to the Jewish community. Their ritual identity falls in the Institutional category and their practice is Traditional (see Figure 3.5).

---

9   French sociologist Émile Durkheim worked on the assumption that civic rituals draw people with differing views together at the inauguration of a ruler but also at a civil wedding ceremony. They generate a sense of community that goes beyond politics and natural alliances.

Aaliyah and Joshua were raised in the Jewish tradition which, as adults, they practise separately and together. Their vital concerns were made special through the unusual language, repetition, exaggerated gestures, formalized or prescribed movements and stylized performance of their wedding ceremony. As the newlyweds pronounced the vows and repeated the gestures of Jewish couples who married before them, they were initiated into married life in that tradition. This felt right and meaningful to Aaliyah and Joshua because it anchored them in their community and its history. It felt right to their non-Jewish guests too because they recognized their friends' life and values in the ceremony (see Figure 3.3).

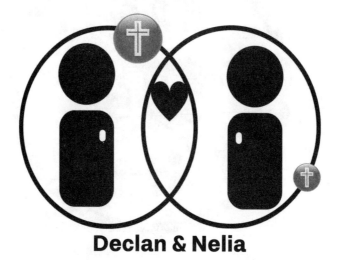

Declan & Nelia

Figure 3.4. Dilemma of contemporary couples
Couples like Declan and Nelia are often confused when it comes to organizing a meaningful wedding ceremony. Technically, they could have had a Catholic wedding but they did not because it did not feel right to them. This figure illustrates why.
In Declan and Nelia's personal areas there is a symbol of a Christian cross. Declan's cross, situated prominently above his head, indicates the tradition's importance in his personal life. Christian influence is less significant for Nelia; her cross is smaller and appears behind her. Since the Christian rite reflects neither what drew the couple together, nor how they expect to nourish their relationship in the future, the cross does not appear in the space between them. The couple's joint ritual identity is 'Distanced' and their joint ritual practice is 'Unaffiliated' (see Figure 3.5).

DILEMMA OF CONTEMPORARY COUPLES

As models for how couples are drawn and held together change sharing the same religious and cultural traditions is no longer considered essential for coupleship, or necessarily an advantage. Like Aaliyah and Joshua, Declan and Nelia were both raised in the same religious tradition. Unlike the Jewish couple, Declan and Nelia do not practise Christianity together (see Figure 3.4). Declan's family put considerable pressure on the couple to have a Catholic wedding.[10] While Declan was comfortable with the idea, it did not feel right to Nelia.[11]

Even when couples with different backgrounds are not denied religious rites outright, the traditional words and gestures may well feel unsuitable or meaningless to them. The chances of finding a ready-to-celebrate ceremony that feels authentic are slim for people like Nelia and Declan. What is a couple to do when traditional rites do not fit?

SENSEMAKING[12] IN RITUALMAKING[13]

Making sense of ritual and making ritual that makes sense has been a challenge across the ages. Beatniks and hippies[14] invented ritual

---

10 Christian churches can be grouped into three different branches: Orthodox, Catholic and Protestant. The Orthodox rite of marriage does not unite a man and a woman but simply shows the church's recognition of the union. In a similar way, the Roman Catholic priest's official role in the marriage ceremony consists only of witnessing the rite as the spouses themselves exchange the bread and wine (Eucharist) and their promise to marry. The Protestant marriage ceremony is a public declaration of love and commitment witnessed by friends and family.

11 By and large, the appropriateness of traditional rites depend on the extent to which the couple find support for their relationship within the established community.

12 Sensemaking is the process by which people make sense of their experiences. While this process has been studied by other disciplines under other names for centuries, the term 'sensemaking' has marked scientific research since the 1970s. It is widely used today in specific social sciences such as philosophy, sociology, cognitive science and especially social psychology and interdisciplinary research programmes.

13 The term 'ritualmaking' refers to the process by which people create rituals to make sense of their life event experiences. Like the word sensemaking, it is now used by researchers and practitioners alike.

14 Alan Watts is quoted as saying '[W]hen somebody comes in from the Orient with a new religion which hasn't got any [horrible] associations in our minds, all the words are new, all the rites are new, and yet, somehow it has feeling in it, and we can get with that, you see, and we can dig that!' (Cohen 1991, n.p.).

performances where 'improvisation, direct experience, immediacy, and spontaneity were priorities' (Aukeman 2016, p.107).

In the post-Flower Power era, Ritual Power branched out with the arrival of wedding planners and non-religious humanist and funeral societies. Non-traditional or 'new' ritual that has not moved beyond the ritual performances of the 1950s and 1960s has got bad press. 'Half a century later, DIY rituals can still be awkward, embarrassing or meaningless' (Grimes 2017).

REPACKAGING RITUAL AS STRATEGY

Ritual is a 'culturally strategic way of acting in the world' (Jonte-Pace 2009).[15] Either traditional rites or new rituals can meet the human need to mark an occasion or life event. Nonetheless, in order for emerging ritual to be effective and meaningful today, it needs a new ritual strategy that involves repackaging with social values that are broader than those of the 1950s and 1960s such as respectfulness, thoughtfulness – and rigour.

First of all, just like traditional ritual, new rituals must take into account how the body experiences the ceremony. Embodied emotions are engaged in the most profound way in ritual. When rituals feel right they can touch the body's 'felt-sense' to effect a 'felt shift' (Gendlin 1962, p.44). Life event rituals need to feel right to be right (Holloway 2015). It is 'impossible to build memories, engage in complex thoughts or make meaningful decisions without emotion... We only think deeply about things we care about' (Immordino-Yang 2016, p.18). Peacebuilder Lisa Schirch promotes the use of ritual when addressing complex, deep-rooted conflicts that require lasting transformation of world views, identities and relationships, because it can help people see each other as human beings rather than as enemies. 'Ritual is a powerful form of communication precisely because it involves people's bodies, senses, and emotions' (Schirch 2005, p.83).

---

15 Ritual studies scholar Catherine Bell's 'profound insight was that ritual, long thought of as thoughtless action stripped of context, is more interestingly understood as strategy: a culturally strategic way of acting in the world. Ritual is a form of social activity' (Jonte-Pace in Bell 2009 [1992], p.vii).

Second, only a ritual context that feels safe can make us feel less alone, more supported, inventive, proactive and alive. We live in a dislocated society at the cusp of an era of inevitable change. The challenges of our ultramodern world require that people everywhere 'do something' to remain human and connected with others. Ritual can provide a framework for expressing and harnessing strong and potentially dangerous emotions in a harmonious and fulfilling manner. Only then can it serve as profoundly humanizing and civilizing force that fixes us – individually and collectively – firmly in present reality.

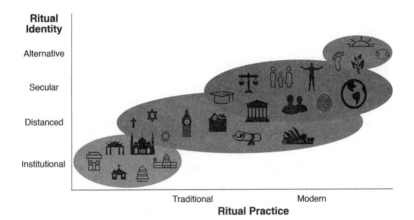

Figure 3.5. Ritual profile: Identity and practice
A coherent ritual profile results in ceremonies that reinforce emotional attunement and the sense of belonging to a community. People with Institutional (religious or civic) identity and practice are usually satisfied with traditional rituals. Those with Secular identity may practise Traditional or non-traditional (Unaffiliated) rituals. People with Alternative identity usually opt for esoteric non-traditional rituals. Couples with Distanced identity and Traditional practice may find what they need in Institutional rites. Those who tend more towards Unaffiliated practice are most at risk for disappointment with rituals that fall short of their fundamental needs.

Third, in order for ritual to mean something the ceremony must be consistent with our values, ritual identity and ritual practice (see Figure 3.5). A traditional wedding ceremony suited Aaliyah and Joshua's needs perfectly. Declan and Nelia needed something different. Ritual works for couples like them when it is unpacked and repackaged to focus on their relationship, and on what the two of them hold most dear in life. Only then will the wedding ceremony feel meaningful to the fiancés – and those to whom the couple may turn to for support – their witnesses, families and friends.

Finally, it is coherence with ritual strategy that determines whether or not rituals work. It is how we make and use new rituals that turn them into a beneficial way of acting in the world. People introduce meaning into the ceremony through their choices about venue, the content of ceremony, who participates and who is invited. When these elements are well chosen they contribute to making sense of the occasion. The practice of meaningful ritual with others in an appropriate setting paves the way for transformation.

RITUAL PRACTICE THAT CELEBRATES LIFE

Ritual that celebrates a life event such as the transition to coupleship or an official union 'serves as a benchmark or reference point among a series of lesser points', affirms ritual anthropologist Matthieu Smyth. 'It reassures us that we have indeed moved on from one phase to another, and that the transition has truly been completed. It inaugurates a new reality within which we can evolve in peace' (Smyth, personal communication 2014). A meaningful wedding ceremony reaches beyond the community witnessing the event to a broader place and time (see Figure 3.2). Guests have a sense of accompanying the couple as they enter a new phase of life. The couple feels married.

Fiancés who are conscious of their ritual profile knowingly choose effective rituals, be they traditional or emerging, as a strategic way of preparing themselves for their future together. Ritual is not a game, but it can be playful; it is not therapy, but it can be therapeutic; it is not theatre, but it is theatrical; it is not art, but it is artistic (see *Notes on Repackaging Ritual*).

WHAT KIND OF CEREMONY?

Having a clear idea about your respective and joint ritual profiles will help you honour your uniqueness as individuals and design a wedding ceremony that reinforces your relationship. Before moving on to Chapter 4, print out two copies of the *Questionnaire on my ritual profile*, one for you and one for your partner. Complete the questionnaires separately. The right answers are the ones the give the best portrait of your ritual profile. The questionnaire should take about 15 minutes.

Choose a setting you both enjoy, settle in comfortably. Now you are ready to share the results of your questionnaires with your partner. Allow at least an hour for this part of the exercise.

- What did you learn about your ritual profile? Do your partner's results reflect what you know about him/her?

- Which aspects of your individual profiles are similar? Which are different?

- How have you marked those special moments in your relationship (see Figure 2.1)?

- What is your joint ritual profile?

- What kind of ceremony do you need to celebrate your coupleship?

TOOLBOX

RITUAL PROFILE
Questionnaire on my ritual profile

This questionnaire is designed to help you define your own ritual profile and determine the best strategy for ritualizing different life events, from birthdays to weddings to funerals.

Part I Circle the icons next to the statements that best describe you and bar those that do not apply.

★ I am an active member of a religious institution.

● I am an inactive member of a religious institution.

■ I am a member of an organization with humanist or philosophical views.

◆ I am attracted to groups which value holistic or esoteric practices.

★ I attend religious worship services at least once a month.

■ I live by my own ethic which is based on reason and humanistic values.

● I attend religious worship services about once or twice a year.

◆ Life is a natural process. My life event ceremony should celebrate the mystery, joy and uncertainty of life.

■ My wedding / funeral / child's life event ceremony could take place almost anywhere, except in a religious setting.

◆ I celebrate nature, am sensitive to the colours of the seasons and marvel at the cosmos.

★ I imagine my wedding / funeral / child's ceremony in a religious setting.

● I would love to have my wedding / funeral / child's life event ceremony in a religious setting but, if possible, without a priest / pastor / rabbi / imam or other religious leader.

■ As human beings, we alone are responsible for solving the environmental problems we have created. No belief in a god or a supernatural force can help us.

◆ It is important for me to have a simple funeral and to be buried or have my ashes spread in a natural setting, far from artificial structures.

★ I cannot imagine my wedding / funeral / child's ceremony without a priest / pastor / rabbi / imam or other religious leader.

● My wedding / child's life event ceremony may be held in a secular setting but I cannot imagine my funeral without religious rites.

◆ A life event ceremony with a shaman would suit me quite well.

● My family and friends would be disappointed if I did not organize a religious ceremony for my wedding / funeral / child.

- ■ I do not need god or any supernatural being in order to live and die well.
- ★ It is important to have sacred texts and religious rites performed at our wedding / my funeral / our children's life event ceremonies.
- ■ I want my wedding / funeral / child's ceremony to be presided by a humanist celebrant or at least someone who shares my humanist values.

Part II Circle the icons next to the statements that best describe you and bar those that do not apply.

- □ Religious holidays are important to me because they preserve my cultural and social traditions.
- △ I advocate progressive values and ideals regarding gender and social roles.
- □ Official documents (religious or civic) confirming my wedding / funeral / child's life events are important to me.
- △ A ceremony which celebrates my wedding / my funeral / my child's life events must correspond to our values rather than to official social or civic standards.
- △ I belong to one or several groups composed of people who come together around projects, leisure activities or ideals.
- □ I am most comfortable with time-tested values, roles and rituals.
- △ I like the idea of having a close friend or non-official person preside over a life event ceremony, such as my wedding, funeral or a naming ceremony for my child.
- □ Only a spiritual or civic leader can validate the ceremony of a life event, such as our wedding, a funeral or a ceremony for our child.
- △ I can imagine holding my wedding / funeral / child ceremony in a unique setting such as a museum, garden, restaurant, library or on a farm.

Part III Please note below the number of times you have ticked each of these six symbols and, if you wish, your observations.

Observations:

★ _____

● _____

■ _____

◆ _____

△ _____

☐ _____

See the *Key to the questionnaire on my ritual profile* in Chapter 4.

 Inventory on ritual profile for weddings

How well do you know your partner and the kind of wedding would s/he want? What is your ritual profile? (See *Questionnaire on my ritual profile*.) The best strategy for ritualizing your union is *influenced* by your separate ritual profiles but firmly *grounded* on the values you share.

Part 1 Circle the statements that best describe **your partner** and bar those that do not apply.

★ S/he is an active member of a religious institution.

● S/he is an inactive member of a religious institution.

■ S/he is a member of an organization with humanist or philosophical views.

◆ S/he is attracted to groups which value holistic or esoteric practices.

● S/he attends religious worship services at least once a month.

■ S/he lives by her/his own ethical code which is based on reason and humanistic values.

★ S/he attends religious worship services about once or twice a year.

◆ S/he wants our wedding ceremony to be romantic, magic, mysterious and aesthetic.

■ S/he would agree that our wedding could take place almost anywhere, except in a religious setting.

◆ S/he celebrates nature, is sensitive to the colours of the seasons and marvels at the cosmos.

★ S/he would want our wedding ceremony held in a religious setting with a religious leader.

● S/he would want our wedding ceremony in a religious setting but, if possible, without a priest / pastor / rabbi / imam or other religious leader.

■ In her/his view, there is absolutely no need for religious approval of our union.

◆ S/he wants a simple wedding reception in a natural setting, far from artificial structures.

★ It is fundamental for my partner that our union be blessed by a priest / pastor / rabbi / imam or other religious leader.

● S/he is not religious but would not object to having our wedding ceremony in a religious setting because she knows it would please me.

◆ A wedding ceremony presided by a shaman would suit her/him quite well.

● Her/his family and friends would object if we did not organize a religious ceremony for our wedding.

■ In her/his view, no god or any supernatural beings are necessary for living and dying well.

★ S/he would want sacred texts read and religious rites performed at our wedding ceremony.

■ S/he would want our wedding ceremony to be presided by a humanist celebrant or at least someone who shares her/his humanist values.

Part II Circle the icons next to the statements that best describe **your partner** and bar those that do not apply.

☐ Religious holidays are important to her/him because they preserve cultural and social traditions.

Δ S/he advocates progressive values and ideals regarding gender and social roles.

☐ Official recognition (social, civic or religious) of our union is important to her/him.

Δ S/he would say that our wedding ceremony must reflect the values we share.

Δ S/he belongs to one or several groups which are composed of people who come together around projects, leisure activities or ideals.

☐ S/he is most comfortable with time-tested values, roles and rituals.

Δ S/he likes the idea of having a close friend or non-official person preside over our wedding.

☐ In her/his view, *it would not feel like a real wedding* without a religious leader.

Δ S/he would love to have our wedding ceremony in a unique setting such as a museum, garden, restaurant, library or on a farm.

Part III Please note below the number of times you have ticked each of these six symbols and, if you wish, your observations.

Observations:

See the *Key to the inventory on ritual profile for weddings* in Chapter 4.

NOTES ON REPACKAGING RITUAL

In view of the many confusing definitions of ritual, it may be quite enough for us to be able to recognize one when we see one. Just as the quality of a photo depends on the contrast of light and shadow, recognizing repackaged ritual depends on having a sense of what it is and what it is not.

ARTISTIC, NOT ART

A simple flower arrangement or tables and chairs set out in a pleasing way reveal a couple's taste and their concern for their guests' comfort. By altering ordinary aspects of our everyday world such as objects, places, sounds and actions we deliberately make them extraordinary. 'Unlike most other concepts of art,[16] artification considers art as an activity and does not require that the results be skilled or beautiful' (Dissanayake 2017, p.161).

AUTHENTICITY, NOT PARODY

Rituals that celebrate coupleship must be coherent with the pair's profound values and shared dreams for the future. Culture has long been enriched by the exchange of ideas, yet borrowing rituals from other people's traditions rarely makes sense and can be seen as disrespectful.

Some of my colleagues are regularly asked to add indigenous rituals to wedding ceremonies. The risk of cultural imperialism is

---

16 'Art for art's sake', or '*l'art pour l'art*', a slogan credited to Théophile Gautier (1811–1872), was a reaction among Western artists against the idea that art had to serve some practical, moral or didactic purpose. It presents art as an independent and well-defined domain in itself that is solely concerned with aesthetics, imagination, enjoyment and the self-expression of the artist. George Sand and Friedrich Nietzsche criticized the slogan, claiming that art 'for art's sake' just does not exist. Postcolonial African writers such as Léopold Senghor and Chinua Achebe consider the phrase a Eurocentric view on art and creation.

high; few couples think of what it means to indigenous peoples to see their rituals used out of context (see People's Path 1993). Ritual studies expert Ronald L. Grimes warns against grafting elements we do not understand into our ceremonies, because we will end up with something that we cannot fully absorb (Grimes, personal correspondence 2016). This is particularly true when it comes to objects and rituals from other traditions that have little or no connection with our own lives. So many layers of meaning will remain hidden from us that it cannot feel genuine. More to the point, we do not need others' rituals to give meaning to our celebrations.

Declaration of war against exploiters of Lakota spirituality
Traditional leaders of several tribes have declared war on those who usurp ritual elements of their spiritual tradition:

> Whereas for too long we have suffered the unspeakable indignity of having our most precious Lakota ceremonies and spiritual practices desecrated, mocked and abused by non-Indian 'wannabes', hucksters, cultists, commercial profiteers and self-styled 'New Age shamans' and their followers... Whereas with horror and outrage we see this disgraceful expropriation of our sacred Lakota traditions has reached epidemic proportions in urban areas... We hereby and henceforth declare war against all persons who persist in exploiting, abusing, and misrepresenting the sacred traditions and spiritual practices of the Lakota, Dakota and Nakota people. (People's Path 1993, n.p.)

CELEBRATION, NOT A PARTY

There is no wedding without a ceremony. A party, without a ceremony or even a ceremonial moment to solemnize the couple's commitment, is not a wedding. A social gathering that is an extension of the ceremony celebrates the couple's long-term commitment and offers the guests an opportunity to manifest their support.

PLAYFUL, NOT A GAME

Ritual is assimilated with play. The wedding ceremony and rituals can be light-hearted and playful. Nonetheless, the couple's pledge is not a game, it is for keeps. As witnesses, the guests are duty bound to support the couple in the years to come.

THERAPEUTIC, NOT THERAPY

Weddings are emotionally charged occasions and the rituals effectively channel the emotions generated during the ceremony in a therapeutic manner. The couple that is expecting a child or facing a serious illness, for example, may find that the ceremony has a particularly salutary effect. Even so, the goal of the ceremony is not its possible benefits, such as healing, feeling more peaceful, resolving family issues or consolidating a couple's relationship. There are other, more direct and efficient, means of dealing with these situations. Ritualizing is often therapeutic, but it should not be confused with therapy.

THEATRICAL, NOT THEATRE

A respectful wedding ceremony is plotted out like the script of a play where the couple's vow is the only obligatory text. The fiancés are not actors, but on this occasion they take centre stage together to make their commitment public. They decide who participates in the ceremony and are clear about what these people will say and do when, where and how. All participation by family members, friends or musicians appears in the libretto; their movements are blocked out like choreographic sequences on a stage. Even though the wedding ceremony is theatrical, it is not theatre.

TIME-OUT-OF-TIME, NOT TIME-OUT

Have you ever walked out of a wedding? Do you know why? In normal circumstances, the brain's timekeeper[17] keeps us conscious of the fact that whatever is happening – good or bad – will sooner or later end. During a well-constructed ceremony, the competent presider ensures a safe context for strong emotions. Feelings may swell, recede and circulate, without bursting the emotional framework of the ceremony. There may be a salutary time-out-of-time feeling: people are present but lose track of time because it seems to accelerate, slow down or be suspended as they live fully in the present. During an event – be it happy or sad – that is too stressful or poorly contained, the brain's timekeeper can go offline.[18] After a stretch, a smile, a yawn or a heaving a sigh of relief, our timekeeper resets, and we return to normal time.

VOLUNTARY, NOT IMPOSED

Rituals must not be foisted on a couple without their input. Guests should not be forced to participate with gestures or words that make them uncomfortable. Avoid these kinds of situation by using your own objects, symbols and language in your wedding ceremony.

---

17 Biologists refer to this observable absence of action as 'freeze'; psychologists, with descriptions of how this sense of absence feels from the inside, talk about 'dissociation'. The scientific name for the timekeeper is the dorsolateral prefrontal cortex (DLPFC). It is responsible for 'telling us how our present experience relates to the past and how it may affect the future' (van der Kolk 2014, p.69).

18 Severed contact with our inner sensate compass is experienced as fragmentation or disembodiment. Neurologist Robert Scaer describes this frightening experience as 'an aberration of memory' (2001, p.43). The inability to live fully in the present impedes adequate preparation for the future which in turn wreaks havoc on health and social relationships such as marriages, families and friendships (Scaer 2005, p.152; 2012, p.114).

PART II

CRAFTING THE CEREMONY

Ritualmaking is a powerful craft that can shape how couples see themselves and transform their future. Part II looks at the basics of ritual craft: planning, creating and realizing. Like all crafts, ritualmaking requires discipline, creativity, a few guidelines, appropriate tools and a good checklist. Crafting a meaningful wedding ceremony is a profoundly human activity that involves the mind, the body and even the viscera, a process that takes the couple to the heart of their reality.

4

PLANNING THE
CEREMONY

On a snowy January evening, Amrita and Joe join their friends around a bright fire at a family ski lodge in the Poconos. 'So, lovebirds, how's the wedding business coming along?' asks Nelia, peeking over her hot chocolate. 'Weddings are definitely a business!' exclaims Joe. 'I can't believe how much time we spend scoping out venues, caterers and photographers... Amrita is constantly on Instagram and blogs...'

'What have you come up with so far?' queries Joshua. 'Well, apart from the date, not much...' sighs Amrita. 'Good venues are hard to come by,' adds Joe. 'The Inn in York County where Declan and Nelia held their reception is booked for our weekend... You already know about the zoo – our first choice for the ceremony venue – you have to reserve it for the whole wedding... On the upside, we got permission to hold a short ceremony in the park on Saturday morning, and Terry is working with us. She's not free on our date, but Tyler has kindly offered to preside...' 'And' smiles Amrita, 'Kayla will be watching from the wings to make sure it all goes to plan.'

'So, your wedding will be like Kayla and Tyler's?' asks Filippa. Amrita and Joe exchange looks, and Kayla exclaims: 'That's impossible! Our ritual strategies are so different.' 'Your what...?' probes Halvar. Kayla replies: 'If Joe and Amrita have the Questionnaire and Inventory on ritual profile, we can make copies and show you. Are you game?'

After the friends complete the questionnaires separately, Tyler presents two diagrams (see Figures 2.1 and 3.5). He explains that a couple's ritual strategy is based on their shared approach to life and ceremonies. The couples spend another 10 minutes identifying their joint ritual strategy.

Tyler then asks the group how they see Aaliyah and Joshua's ritual strategy. 'That's easy,' says Declan: 'Their strategy for their wedding involved a religious ceremony because their joint ritual profile is "Institutional" and their practice is "Traditional"' (see Figure 3.3). 'Close', corrects Joshua, 'I'm much less traditional than Aali. That ceremony involved more negotiation than you'd think. I'd like to hear about your results...' Nelia replies: 'We're both "Distanced" from religion; Declan is more traditional than I am' (see Figure 3.4). Declan adds: 'Looking at those two diagrams, Tyler, I understand better why our civil ceremony felt empty.'

'Tyler, what about you two? You are clearly "Secular", but what about Kayla? She's more...ah...spiritual,' says Basie. Kayla says: 'You all know that I lived in Jamaica till I was 15, raised in turn by my Rastafarian father and Hindu grandmother. This suggests an "Alternative" identity with "Unaffiliated" practice. But I'm not my past. I'm a scientist who senses that objects, places and creatures have a spiritual essence. A spiritual humanist perhaps?... (see Figure 4.1). That's why our strategy involved a homemade humanist ceremony; nothing else would have fit us. I'm curious to know what you and Paul came up with.'

Paul glances at Basie before saying: 'We didn't think this exercise would apply to us at all. Our backgrounds, professional interests and friends are very different. We don't go to church but we do a lot of cultural, social and sporty activities together. While we're fine with "Secular" identity, the Traditional practice results surprised us. Our strategy for ritualizing our partnership? It's true we're considering marriage...but laws won't hold us together' (see Figure 4.2).

Filippa stands up and yawns, 'Listen, Halvar and I have to get back to the baby and the sitter. But before we go, I want to say that, not being married or religious, we didn't think this was for us either. Yet respect of, and responsibility for, what Kayla calls the "essence of things" is important to us. In Sweden, it's illegal to build a fire on or next to a rock because the heat can crack it or cause disfiguring scars that never heal... We drew rocks, meals, skiing, Swedish holidays (flag) and family in that special place we share with Thor; we make ordinary things special all the time... That's our strategy (see Figure 4.3). Can we continue this discussion at breakfast?'

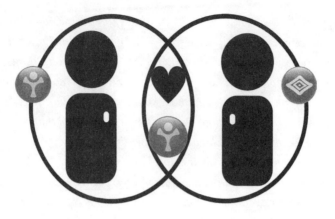

Figure 4.1. Tyler & Kayla
Tyler and Kayla's shared concern for humanist values is represented by a humanist symbol in the space they share. The arbitrary symbol known as 'eye of the spirits' in Kayla's personal space denotes her 'Alternative' approach to spirituality. Their joint ritual profile is 'Secular'.

Figure 4.2. Basie & Paul
Basie and Paul are a non-traditional and multicultural couple. Their relationship is enriched by their enjoyment of opera, sports and costume parties, joint volunteer and eco-building projects and their dog Rusty. Basie admired his father's dedication to the Black Muslims but did not share his interest. He enjoys horseback riding. Paul was raised in a non-religious expat family in France; he likes water sports. As from 2015, LGBT couples living in the United States can legally marry but Paul's current professional situation makes it unwise for the couple to do so at this time.

Figure 4.3. Filippa & Halvar
Filippa and Halvar, a Swedish couple temporarily posted in New York, share the same culture and family traditions. This is symbolized in the diagram by the Swedish flag that covers their separate spaces and the space they share. Their relationship is represented by that middle space filled with the activities and people they care about. They feel no social or cultural pressure to be legally married but are planning a ceremony in nature (pile of stones) to welcome their son Thor into the family. They feel most comfortable with 'Secular' ritual identity and 'Unaffiliated' ritual practice.

Wedding trends shift quickly today. Fiancés now opt for autumn rather than spring celebrations, making October the new May. The wedding must be unique and memorable – not only for the couple but also for their families and friends.

PERSONALIZATION AND THE ULTIMATE EXPERIENCE

A poll of nearly 13,000 brides and grooms points to a rising trend towards 'total personalization' and the 'ultimate guest experience' (Knot 2016). Around 40 per cent of the couples interviewed say they felt pressure from the media to have the 'perfect' wedding (up 20% from ten years ago). This means weddings that are pricier than ever. Like Joe and Amrita, many couples assume about half of the often considerable cost of the wedding.

Wedding fashions – and following the trends – make for a thriving business. Media pressure alone accounts for a 300 per cent increase in the hiring of wedding planners. In spite of support from planners, much of the fiancés' time is spent scoping out potential vendors such as floral designers, dress designers, make-up artists, photographers, venues, caterers, not to mention entertainers for the reception. Moreover, couples are expected to perform for blogs and online bridal publications which, incidentally, are vendors' best source for clients (Gontcharova 2017).

A more recent survey of over 15,000 couples suggests that many couples intentionally choose the more expensive route. They crop the guest list (from 120 to 110) and spend more money per guest (WeddingWire 2017) to create the 'ultimate guest experience' with out-of-the-box[1] entertainment, from comedians, jugglers, illusionists, fire breathers, aerialists and circus performers to LED robots, food trucks, lawn games, photo and tattoo booths, casino tables and live portrait artists. While #cheap or #low-cost weddings appears an oxymoron there is growing interest in green weddings (see *Notes on totally personalizing your ceremony* and *Notes on the ultimate guest experience*).

Despite hype and new trends, some things do not change. Now, as in the past, Joe and Amrita's alliance involves at least three family groups: the couple's new family unit and their families of origin. The ceremony they choose and their wedding rituals reveal their upbringing, values, spirituality and social situation. Whether they have a simple reception or shell out the equivalent of a year's salary for an unforgettable party, it contributes to acceptance of their new marital status and reinforces ties with family and friends.

So, why expend so much money, time and energy? How did we get to the 'total personalization' and the 'ultimate guest experience' wedding?

---

1   The Urban Dictionary (2018) cites three definitions for 'out-of-the box': (1) Something that is part of the product, no customization needed. (2) Nonconformal [sic] creative thinking. (3) Something or somebody that is exceptional or unusually good. All three apply to the usage here.

DEPERSONALIZATION AND DISLOCATION

Depersonalized interactions with people and unrelenting pressure towards individualism and competition deprive us of our individuality and dislocate[2] us from social life (Alexander 2018). Fewer and fewer people serve others directly, repair things or even make their own food. Bank tellers are replaced by ATMs and shopkeepers by automated checkouts. A doctor's clinical observations – including taste, smell and touch – are supposedly rendered obsolete by test tubes and scanners. Walking with our heads and eyes down, we 'chat' with our thumbs from virtual bubbles that make it hard to wed – or even meet – real people.

RECONNECTING WITH OURSELVES AND OTHERS

Satisfying intimate relationships are a fundamental human need. When we consciously reenact ancient social practices around commitment such as courtship, the proposal and the wedding, feelings of connection and belonging are enhanced. The 'total personalization' wedding may well be interpreted as the couple's desire to reconnect with themselves and others on physical and emotional levels. The 'ultimate guest experience' represents an effort to restore the fine structure lattice of the couple's 'community'.

Couples who understand what is behind their need for personalization and their desire to offer their guests a memorable experience take a totally different approach to planning their wedding. Crafting a custom wedding ceremony is the acme of total personalization. Moreover, it is a 'must' for all but couples who practice the same religious tradition – and even they ask for personalized touches nowadays (Le Roux 2018). The quintessential guest experience involves creating a setting with activities that facilitate real interaction between the couple and their guests as well as among the guests.

---

2   In chemistry, the term 'dislocation' refers to irregularities in the fine structure lattice of an otherwise normal crystal. In this context the word refers to subtle and not so subtle irregularities in the fine structure lattice of modern society.

CHECKLIST FOR A WEDDING CEREMONY

PLANNING
First things first

☐ We are clear about our objectives for this ceremony

We have identified:

☐ **About whom?** Couple

☐ **By whom?** The couple are responsible for crafting/presiding/organizing

☐ **With whom?** (who **participates/is invited**)

☐ **What?** Wedding ceremony

☐ **When?** A fitting **date/time/duration** for the event

☐ **Where?** A suitable **place/setting/venue**

COMMUNICATION AND CONTINGENCY

☐ We have contacted or invited all (see 'With whom?') noted above

☐ Participants have approved their roles

☐ If there is disagreement about how to proceed we know who makes the final decision

☐ We have contingency plans for with Whom, When and Where

PAUSE

CREATING
Making sense (couple)

We, the craftspeople, are agreed on:

☐ **Why and how** we are ritualizing our union

☐ Our vow is at the **HEART ♥** of this ceremony

☐ The **key values**, ideals or **philosophy of life** we wish to transmit or convey

☐ **Confirm consistency of choices** (Who, What, When, Where) with values

☐ In case of disagreement, we have discussed the issues

CONTENT

☐ **Words ♥ Our vow + texts**

☐ **Music**

☐ **Gestures/symbols/objects**

FORMAT

☐ **Entry** into ceremonial space

☐ **Welcome**

☐ **Heart ♥ Our vow+ texts**

☐ **Closing/exit** ceremonial space > transition

☐ **Social gathering**

☐ **Choreography/scenography** check for visual participation from all seats

☐ **Reminder list**

☐ **We have walked through the ceremony and checked for flow and choreography**

PAUSE

REALIZING
Expressing meaning

☐ **Prepare setting** (couple/presider/organizer)

☐ **Open ceremony** (presider)

☐ **Ritualizing** (Content + Format)

   ♦ Conduct (presider) ♦ Participate (all)

☐ **Close ceremony** (presider)

☐ **Open social part of event** (organizer)

☐ **Social gathering** (all)

☐ **Close event and clean up** (organizer)

DURATION OF EVENT (suggested)

Ceremony (20–40 minutes)

Social gathering (2–6 hours)

CRAFTING THE CUSTOM CEREMONY

A custom wedding ceremony is, by definition, one of a kind. It has never been done before and will never be done again. Organizing a wedding can be all absorbing to the point of testing the patience of the most mature couple.

Allot 6 to 12 months for crafting your wedding ceremony. A well-crafted ceremony begins with good **planning** of who, where and when. Establish a calendar of tasks by working backwards from your wedding date. This way you know that, if you begin crafting your ceremony six months before your big day, you have three to four weeks to write your vow.

During the **creating** phase you will explore the Why and How of the ceremony. Give yourselves the time you need – four to six months – to clarify your shared profile, values and common goals – and permission to change your mind. This last advice may save you time in the long run.

As you go along, try to visualize yourselves during the ceremony in the setting you have chosen. Get into the habit of walking it through in your mind. Imagine how the words and gestures might feel to you on the day of your wedding. Most couples find that the weeks running up to their wedding day are filled with unexpected details that only they can sort out, such as where *will* Aunt Mathilda stay?! Keep last minute stress to a minimum by putting the finishing touches on your ceremony six to eight weeks before the big day.

The final phase, **realizing**, absorbs lots of intense energy, but it takes comparatively very little time. A well-constructed wedding ceremony lasts 20–40 minutes. The realizing phase involves setting up, the ceremony itself, the social gathering and clean-up.

Last but not least, practical knowledge of ritualmaking requires some basic tools. 'People need new Tools to work with rather than new Tools that work for them,' exclaimed Ivan Illich (1973, p.10). Pertinent tools for contemporary ritualizing are introduced in each of the three phases: planning, creating and realizing.

PLANNING PHASE

The planning phase begins early, especially for fiancés who want a popular venue. Answering the questions in the planning phase – What, Who, When and Where – may take you a few minutes, or much longer. Your answers to these questions need to be confirmed during the creating phase. After you have had a chance to identify what is at the heart of your ceremony you will be asked to reexamine these choices and test their consistency in light of your goals and values. This extra step is a safeguard that ensures your choices correspond to your ritual strategy and needs.

Don't forget to take regular breaks between the different phases of the crafting process. Your ideas need time to settle. Give yourselves permission to say: STOP, I need a rest! Respect this decision by setting a date and time for your next discussion. Then, take a walk, go to the gym or move on to another activity.

For your first planning session, set aside an hour in a comfortable setting.

MATERIALS NEEDED

Your respective agendas. A sheet of paper for notes. Writing implements.

INSTRUCTIONS

Go through the questions in the first column and make a list of the main questions: What, Who, When, Where. Note the aspects you have already settled, your preferences and options.

Make a list of things to do, such as people or places to contact.

Start your guest list with names of your closest family members and friends. Count the number of guests. Only then consult others, such as your parents, to see who might have been left out. It is your wedding; you have the right to negotiate the guest list. The *Prioritizing* tool may be useful here.

Determine if you want outside help for the next phase, the creating process. If so, interview a few people and decide together who would best suit the two of you.

Set a date for your next discussion. Between sessions, keep talk about wedding plans to a minimum.

QUESTIONS FOR THE PLANNING PHASE
Who? / What?

Your relationship is the living entity at the centre of your marriage (see Figure 2.1). Both of you are responsible for nourishing it and keeping it alive. In the same way, the two of you are co-responsible for keeping your relationship at the heart of your wedding ceremony.

As craftspeople you are also your main resource: who you are, your shared hopes and fears, your ties to your guests, your joint life experience, books you have read, films you appreciate, food you like to eat, anything and everything that has meaning to you in this context makes for rich material in ritualmaking.

People close to you – family members and friends – also participate in essential, but secondary, roles during your ceremony. Most of your close friends and family will feel honoured to be asked to be involved in your wedding. Speaking, in particular, can feel like a burden to family and friends who have to guess what texts or symbols might please the two of you. During the creating phase you will learn how to write texts your loved ones can read and craft rituals in which they can participate. This facilitates their task but also ensures that your ceremony reflects your dreams for the future and how you see your relationship – rather than what others think you should wish for and be.

Your guests participate in the wedding not only through speech and gestures but also by their presence. Active and passive participants will use all of their senses to experience and make sense of your wedding rituals.

When?

When is the best date and time for your ceremony? Is there a date that marks an important chapter in your relationship? Perhaps there is an hour of the day that is significant for the two of you. You cannot book your ideal venue and take in to account everyone's holiday plans, so there is no sense in sending a Doodle to 200 potential guests. Check with a few key people like parents, grandparents, siblings and those you want in your wedding party to make sure they are free to participate.

Where?

When choosing a wedding venue consider not only the physical aspects but also how this place fits in with your life as a couple. What makes the setting for the ceremony special to you? How about the space occupied by people? Consider the place of every object you bring into the space where the ritual. Are these chairs, table, flowers or arch necessary? Do they contribute or detract from the ceremony? Maybe you need only a few chairs for close family members. One row of chairs or benches may suffice to delimit the ceremonial space. The suitability of the objects depends not on custom but on what makes sense and is coherent with the essence of your ceremony.

The venue for your wedding should feel comfortable to both of you in every way, including cost. Is the setting adapted to the kind of activities you planned? Can your programme proceed in the venue in fair and foul weather? Make sure you have a Plan B that satisfies you both too. Consider ecological issues related to the venue such as travel distance, decorations and catering (see the end of this chapter). Is the venue accessible and safe for all of the guests you invited (elderly, disabled and small children)?

PAUSE

RISK FACTORS FOR THE PLANNING PHASE

The greatest risk in this first phase lies in unexpressed, and thus unmet, expectations. Misunderstandings are often due to lack of communication or to giving people unsuitable roles. Leave time for the unexpected. If you plan an outdoor ceremony have contingency plans for inclement weather.

TOOLBOX

TOOLS FOR THE PLANNING PHASE

The toolbox contains basic tools for the planning phase of crafting wedding rituals.

Seven destressing techniques. See tools in Chapter 1.

Ritual Profile. See tools in Chapter 3.

Checklist for the Wedding Ceremony

There is something remarkably reassuring about lists. Lists appear simple, often deceptively so. A child can use a list to pick up things for his parents from the corner store. Students, business people, factories and bus companies use agendas, schedules or some form of a timetable to keep track of commitments and deadlines. A person with a failing memory can follow a list to remind herself of her daily routine.

Checklists are required for success, affirms surgeon Atul Gawande (2011, p.79). He distinguishes between three kinds of problems: the simple, the complicated and the complex. Whether one is building a basic bookcase, a complicated rocket to go to the moon or a complex skyscraper, Gawande insists that the really important things in life should not be left to memory, or to chance.

The checklist developed by Boeing for airline pilots does not tell pilots how to do their job but simply focuses their attention on a few essential points. Applying this same successful procedure to his domain, Gawande made a *Surgical safety checklist* for the World Health Organization. Like Boeing's list it asks team members to introduce themselves to each other and then agree – together, in advance – what is to be done and who takes control if things go belly-up. When it was tested in eight pilot medical centres around the world, major complications for surgical patients fell 36 per cent and mortality dropped by 47 per cent.

Imagine the success of a medicament – exempt of side-effects – effective on this scale!

Under conditions of complexity such as landing an aircraft, operating on a heart or ritualizing a life event, checklists are not optional for success. The *Checklist for a wedding ceremony* undergirds the three-phase creative process of ritualmaking proposed in this book because it helps keep the fiancés on track. This checklist for weddings got one couple to fix their attention on writing their vows, and let their divorced parents decide who would sit next to whom. While a checklist is no substitute for common sense and skill, and it does not list everything one should do, it does guide the couple as they identify what is at the heart of their ceremony. It obliges them to pause, reflect and dream. The true beauty of the checklist lies in how it makes a couple communicate and assume responsibility – and credit – for the end results.

READ–DO checklists

The list used in this practical guide is referred to as a READ–DO checklist. Each of the three columns in the checklist evokes an action in the crafting process: plan (see Chapter 4), create (see Chapter 5) and realize (see Chapter 6).

The essential elements are identified, listed and then put together in a certain order.

Function of wedding ceremony checklist

1. *Identify the essential elements* and accomplish the main steps needed to plan, create and realize the ceremony.

2. *Enforce pauses* during which the couple talk to each other about what is at the heart of the occasion FOR THEM.

3. Help the couple identify themselves as the craftspeople of their ceremony (a) to *feel like a team* in this creative process, (b) to *decide together in advance* what to do and (c) *who takes control if things do not go as planned.*

4. Ensure that other *lists are made and used* (e.g. wedding list: bridal bouquet, programme, rings...).

Risk factors in using a checklist

While the efficacy of the checklist has been proven time and again, using checklists seems to go against a myth about how successful people function: the truly great are daring, they improvise, they do not need protocols and checklists. 'Maybe our idea of heroism needs updating,' concedes Gawande (2011, p.173). Checklists do impose restrictions: they require personal initiative, discipline and humility. On the upside, lists allow for autonomy and a sense of security in complex situations. In the process of ritualizing a commitment, the list lets the couple focus on the experience. Use the checklist. A checklist only works if it is used.

Who presides?

As a rule of thumb, do not preside your own wedding. Ceremonies presided by newlyweds often resemble a selfie: their emotions appear frozen, the shutter-clicker's eyes and attention are focused elsewhere. Having someone you trust hold the framework of the ceremony leaves you free to be fully present to each other as you pronounce your wedding vow. It is important that the two of you both feel genuinely supported, so make sure you choose this this person together.

The presider's supporting role resembles that of a midwife.[3] The midwife accompanies and assists a mother as she goes into labour and brings her child into the world. Whether the person who presides at the ceremony is a professional or an amateur, the objective is to ensure that the ceremony proceeds as planned and that those at the centre are shown to best advantage (see Figure 4.4 and Table 4.1).

---

3   The term 'midwife' is composed of 'mid', an obsolete Middle English preposition meaning 'with', and 'wif', or woman. In French, a midwife is known as a *sage femme*, which means 'wise woman'.

= Couple + relationship at the centre

= Close family & friends

= Participants (active and passive)

= Presider

Figure 4.4. Main roles for a wedding ceremony
The couple's relationship is at the centre of the ritual. They have the main role in the wedding ceremony. The couple's families and friends are invited as guests and witnesses. Some of their guests may be asked to participate actively by greeting other guests, with a reading or music, in the organization of the event or by presiding the ceremony. The presider is responsible for holding the framework of the ceremony and making sure all goes to plan.

The professional's role

The accompaniment of a professional celebrant is particularly constructive in the planning and creating phases. If there is no professional celebrant available, use the tools in this guide with a coach, or even a psychotherapist, to help you get to the essence of your relationship. It is inadvisable to work on the planning and creating phases with close friends or family members.

You may ask a professional, or a friend or family, to preside your ceremony. Out of respect for the friend or family member, make sure the script for your ceremony is complete, the format is clear and the scenography is spelled out in detail.

Professional support is indicated for all three phases in the following cases:

- you are seriously ill, newly employed or unemployed or facing a crisis

- your or your partner's ritual identity is 'Institutional' or 'Distanced'

- you face family resistance to your plan for a secular ceremony

- you suspect that your values or vision of the future are quite different from those of your partner.

Basic tips on choosing a celebrant or presider

- Do your homework. Decide exactly what you need and what you want the person you are considering to do: accompany you in the planning and creating phases? conduct the ceremony? all three? (see Table 4.1).

- Be wary of letting anyone who might steal the show (professional or nonprofessional) accompany you or preside your ceremony.

- Before interviewing a professional: (1) Check their professional training, accreditation and celebrant's network; (2) Clear up as many questions as possible by telephone or email (availability, services offered, extra fee for distance – if travel is required).

- During the interview: (1) Ask the celebrate to run through the process of crafting a ceremony; (2) How is the content of the ceremony determined? (If the professional supplies a set script, you will work less but *you will not* get a custom ceremony; (3) Ask for details about what the rate covers (limit on number of meetings, telephone or email exchanges? onsite rehearsal?).

- Hire only a celebrant who fits your basic criteria (good first impression, professionalism, availability). Fees vary greatly from region to region. As with most services, the least expensive is not always the best choice. Experienced professionals who help their clients craft bespoke ceremonies must charge higher rates; typically they invest 20–40 hours in accompaniment and presiding a ceremony.

- Trust your instincts!

- The person you choose to preside at your ceremony must be able to put the focus on you and your objectives for the ceremony, provide timely advice and support you unconditionally on this special occasion.

The three columns in Table 4.1 present three roles, goal and requirements one might expect from the person presiding a special occasion. Theoretically, fiancés can be at the centre of and preside their own wedding (see last column) but this is not advisable. They can however easily assume this role at a celebration of their engagement, wedding anniversaries and other life events.

TABLE 4.1. WHAT DOES PRESIDING INVOLVE?

	PROFESSIONAL CELEBRANT	AMATEUR ARTISAN	PERSON AT CENTRE
GOAL			
	Accompany *others* as they ritualize a life event	Ritualize a transition or event for a loved one *(e.g. wedding)*	Ritualize a transition in *their* relationship or life event
REQUIREMENTS			
Professional training	Hands-on celebrant training required	Experience an advantage	None necessary
Public speaking	Experience required; ability to hold an audience	Experience an advantage	Authenticity is most important
Role	Supportive leadership and accompaniment	Secondary; accompaniment	Central
Approach to preparation of the ceremony	Respectful, professional *(priority: clients' desires, needs and interests)*	Disciplined	Disciplined
Values expressed in ceremony	Respect for values of the couple	Respect for values of the couple	Consistent with own values
Presence	Calm presence	Reassuring presence	Involved presence
Attitude	Client-centred: What does this event mean to you (couple)?	Centred on couple: What *does* (not *should*) this event mean to them?	What does this event mean to us?
Emotions	Responsible for interests of the couple; maintains professional distance	Looks after interests of the couple, then own needs	Meet own needs, desires and interests
Reasonable expectations	Conduct ceremony with sensitivity and competence; ability to deal with unexpected incidents	Conduct the ceremony	Preside engagement or anniversary party, but not wedding

Prioritizing

This tool helps visualize who and what are most important, whether that be a relationship or a venue. Prioritizing helps you decide who will be invited to your wedding, where to hold your ceremony and who participates in the ceremony. This exercise can be done alone or with your partner. It takes about 20 minutes.

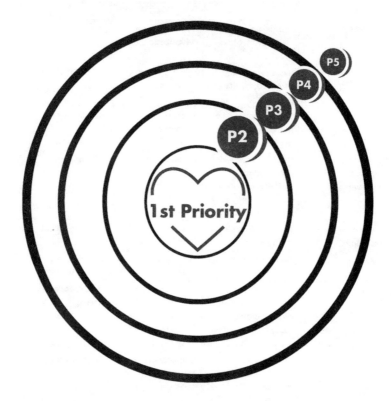

Figure 4.5. How to prioritize
This tool is useful for determining your priorities.

Materials needed

Enlargement of Figure 4.5, writing materials and tracing paper.

First round

This round is about expectations – yours and others. Place tracing paper on top of Figure 4.5. Add the names of the people you are expected to be close to, or options you think you should choose in P1 – this represents your inner circle or top choices and priorities. P2 is your second circle. Place less important people and options in sections P3, P4 and P5. Take a picture of the diagram and label it 'Version A'.

Second round

This round is about feelings. Identify the people you feel close to, or the options that feel right. Take a picture and label it 'Version B'. If this version resembles Version A, you know that you are on the right track. Skip the third round. You are ready to choose who you want to actively participate in your ritualization (people from P1, and perhaps from P2). Determine who will be invited to participate by their presence (people in P2 and P3, for example). If your versions are quite different, take it to another round.

Third round

This round is about compromise. Obligations, our budget, what we want and what we need do not always match up. Compare versions A and B. What is it about this person or option that makes it difficult for you decide? What creative solutions are there for your situation?

Example 1: Too many guests!

Amrita and Joe have too many guests on their list; they do not know how to handle Amrita's mother's demands about inviting her extended family.

In round one, Amrita's mother and her extended family appear in P1. Joe's smaller family and Amrita's father's family are in P2. Their friends are in P3.

The situation feels out of control to the couple. They feel like are helpless bystanders watching from the sidelines. They illustrate this by placing themselves in P4 on the diagram.

In the next round, the couple place themselves in squarely in P1. Amrita's father, a reassuring presence, is in P2. They ask Amrita's father for advice. He encourages them to invite everyone to the wedding ceremony and cocktail and have a more intimate reception. Amrita's father then speaks with his ex-wife and an ex-brother-in-law who works on susceptibilities with that side of the family.

Example 2: Venue crisis

Joe and Amrita were engaged at the New York zoo and would really like to have their ceremony there too. They plan a Friday evening ceremony and cocktail followed by a quiet reception dinner just with their families that evening. On Saturday evening they would like to have a livelier party with friends.

In round one, having their ceremony and cocktail at the zoo falls in P1. The option of another zoo nearby is in P2. A venue nearby in Central Park is option P3. In the process they come across, and fall in love with, the Rare Book Room at the Morgan Library. It seems fitting since Amrita is a librarian, they both enjoy reading and it's not far from where they live and work. But it is not an ideal spot for their ceremony... so, it's in P5.

In round two, after checking out a number of zoo venues online, they see that most, including the Central Park zoo, require booking the whole event there (ceremony, cocktail and reception). Even if they reduce the guest list to a minimum the cost is prohibitive. The nearby zoos have the same rules and cost remains a dissuasive factor. A small private zoo in a nearby state proposes their venue for a more reasonable fee but transporting both families there would be complicated, so it is in P5...

In round three, they realize that the compromise proposed by Amrita's father, with two separate venues, could solve their guest list and budget problems. They plan a trousseau tea with their parents and older relatives on Friday afternoon and their ceremony in Battery Park on Saturday morning, followed by a cocktail brunch for 150 guests at the SeaGlass Carousel. They reserve the Morgan Library for an evening reception with 80 of their nearest family members and closest friends. On Sunday morning they opt for informal activities in order to spend time with friends and the younger set of out-of-town relatives.

 Key to the questionnaire on my ritual profile

What is your ritual profile? Being clear about your ritual profile helps you determine your ritual strategy. A coherent strategy is essential for designing, creating and implementing appropriate rituals that celebrate your life events.

These symbols are indicators of your ritual profile:

- ★ (5)* *Institutional.* If this symbol ★ represents the majority of your answers, your religious practice is regular and satisfying. A religious ceremony would be important for you and consistent with your values and view of life. You probably also ticked this symbol □.

- ● (5) *Distanced.* A majority of this symbol ● indicates occasional religious practice; your ties with a religious institution may be stretched. A ceremony held with a religious leader in a traditional setting may or may not satisfy your need to mark a life event. You may also have ticked the symbol ★. A clear majority of this symbol □ indicates a personalized religious ceremony would be appropriate; a majority of this symbol Δ points to a personalized ceremony outside a religious context.

- ■ (6) *Secular or Humanist.* A majority of this symbol ■ indicates that you identify yourself as a 'none' (e.g. atheist, agnostic). You may be indifferent or even against religion. You may be a member of a humanist or secular group. Tailor-made or humanist ceremonies would best serve your need to mark a life event. You may have a majority of either of these symbols Δ □.

- ◆ (5) *Alternative.* If you ticked this symbol ◆ at least three times it means you find yourself most comfortable with a holistic approach to life and may be a member of an esoteric group. A bespoke ceremony would suit you well. If you ticked a majority of this symbol Δ consider an alternative to a ceremony presided by a traditional authority figure.

These two symbols Δ ☐ can help you fine-tune your ritual profile:

☐   (4) *Traditional*. Cultural and social activities linked to one or more traditions are important to your sense of identity. Yet, feeling strong ties with a tradition neither precludes nor indicates a desire for custom ritual or ceremony. However, when ritualising an occasion, you may need to hear some traditional phrases or to perform certain traditional gestures. It is likely that you ticked a number of these symbols ★ ● ■ , but improbable that you have a majority of this symbol ◆.

Δ   (5) *Modern*. You feel comfortable with people who respect your personal journey and who encourage you in the development of your own values. You may belong to groups with little official status and avoid institutional settings. It is important that you feel free to craft the kind of rituals that are right for you. While you may have ticked a number of these symbols ● ■ ◆ , it is unlikely that you have a majority of this symbol ★.

Indicates the maximum number of times this symbol appears in the questionnaire.

Key to the inventory on ritual profile for weddings

These symbols are indicators of *how you perceive* your partner's ritual profile:

★   (5)* *Institutional.* A majority of this symbol ★ means you see your partner's religious practice as regular and satisfying to her/him. A religious wedding ceremony may be important to her/him and coherent with her/his values and view of life. You probably also ticked this symbol □ a few times.

●   (5) *Distanced.* A majority of this symbol ● indicates that you see your partner's religious practice as occasional. Her/his ties with a religious institution may be stretched. S/he may or may not feel the need to have the wedding ceremony in a religious setting. If you also ticked the symbol ★, pay close attention to how s/he reacts to the statements with these symbols △ □.

■   (6) *Secular or Humanist.* A majority of this symbol ■ indicates that you identify your partner as a 'none' (e.g. atheist, agnostic). S/he may be indifferent or even against religion. S/he may be a member of a humanist or secular group. A tailor-made or humanist wedding ceremony may be a good choice for marking your union. You may have ticked a majority of either of these symbols △ □.

◆   (5) *Alternative.* If this symbol ◆ was ticked at least three times it means you see your partner as being most comfortable with a holistic approach to life. S/he may be a member of an esoteric group. A bespoke wedding ceremony would suit her/him. If you ticked a majority of this symbol △ consider an alternative to a wedding presided by a traditional authority figure.

These two symbols △ □ can help you fine-tune how you see your partner's ritual practice:

□   (4) *Traditional.* You see cultural and social activities linked to one or more traditions as being important to her/his ritual practice. Yet, feeling strong ties with a tradition does not exclude a desire for custom ritual or ceremony. Ask her/him if s/he wants to hear some traditional phrases or perform certain traditional gestures.

It is likely that you ticked a number of these symbols ★ ● ■; a majority of this symbol ◆ is improbable.

Δ   (5) *Modern*. You perceive your partner as prioritizing her/his personal journey and values. S/he may belong to groups with little official status and avoid institutional settings. It would probably be most meaningful for her/him to craft personalized wedding rituals. While you may have ticked a number of these symbols ● ■ ◆ , it is unlikely to have a majority of this symbol ★ .

* Indicates the maximum number of times this symbol appears in the inventory.

How do you *perceive* your partner's ritual profile? What is your own ritual profile? Compare how your partner sees you with how you see yourself. What ritual profile do you share? Your love is showcased in the wedding ceremony when it reveals your shared values and what is important to the two of you. A joint ritual strategy is essential for designing, creating and implementing appropriate rituals to celebrate your union.

NOTES ON TOTALLY PERSONALIZING YOUR CEREMONY

Your ceremony is a showcase for your relationship and you are the stars of the day. Your guests gather to hear you pronounce your vows and celebrate this special occasion with you. While they may know one or both of you, rarely do all the guests know each other. Nothing draws guests together and breaks the ice more effectively than the simple beauty of a fitting wedding ceremony.

COMFORT

Yours

Most couples intend to fully enjoy their big day. Looking back, many find it was unnecessarily stressful. Anticipate the kind of physical and emotional space you will need in the hours up to the ceremony. It is better to have nothing to do than to be rushing around until the last minute. Arrive early, well before the guests. Ensure that the venue is set up as you intended. Go over the details one last time with your celebrant or presider, then let him/her receive the musicians, brief the photographer and check the sound system. Delegate other tasks too such as greeting the guests. Now do what you need to do to feel ready: hang around, chat with people, be alone...or all of the above.

Guests

Your guests' physical and emotional comfort is a priority. Some of the people in your entourage may be uncomfortable with the idea of a non-traditional ceremony or venue. Receive your guests at the ceremony venue with a personal touch. A warm welcome from people they recognize as friends and family will put them immediately at ease. Even an experienced wedding planner and the most competent hotel staff cannot replace greeters.

During the summer months, or spells of warm weather, it is advisable to have water or fruit juice available for guests to prevent dehydration. Do not serve alcoholic drinks before the ceremony. First of all, because these beverages are traditionally reserved for toasting the newlyweds' commitment. Second, serving even one glass of wine before the ceremony signals 'party time' to guests: people tend to talk more loudly and become less attentive to instructions and the setting.

Keep the ceremony short, not more than 40 minutes. An outdoor ceremony should be even more concise, no more than 20–30 minutes. Ensure that guests are well protected from the heat, the cold, direct sunlight and wind. Beware of popping surprises on your guests or giving any speaker carte blanche. It could go well or cause you and your guests considerable discomfort. Improvisation has its place – at the reception.

GREETERS

Hand-pick four to five friends or family members that you would like to honour with this PR task. Your greeters could be people who are too shy to appreciate an active role in the ceremony but great with one-on-one contact. They should not have another role that might interfere with this one, such as dressing the bride or getting the groom to the venue on time.

Brief greeters about what you expect of them. They should familiarize themselves with the facilities, seating arrangements and know where guests should leave coats and gifts. Give your greeters a copy of the guest list. Between them, they should be able to recognize nearly all of your guests and welcome them, if not by name, at least in a language the guest speaks. They may distribute programmes. The celebrant should able to count on them to inform her/him of late arrivals and for helping coordinate the fiancés arrival and the entrance of the wedding party. Their role ends once the ceremony begins.

VENUE

A venue that has significance for you will also be meaningful to your guests. When choosing your venue consider a non-profit organization or a space that could benefit from your event, such as a museum, a cultural organization or an art gallery. If you go that route, ask how the site will use your fee. Would it be for new programmes, upkeep or to enhance the institution's volunteer programme? If you opt for an outdoor ceremony remember to have a Plan B for inclement weather. A botanical garden, arboretum or the grounds of a historic home may have a greenhouse or a covered veranda to keep you and your guests warm and dry.

REDUCING WASTE

Wedding celebrations typically produce significant quantities of rubbish and waste materials. Few wedding organizers aim at zero waste: 'How many times are we going to get married?!' 'So what if our carbon imprint[4] is high, just this once...' You don't need to be a tree-hugging environmentalist to reduce waste. It makes sense not only for the planet, but for us all. Take up the challenge by using your imagination and creativity to concentrate on just one area where you will effectively reduce waste.

INVITATIONS

Although snail mail is still the best option for sending out wedding invitations, paperless save-the-date announcements are becoming more common. Lend a personal touch to your save-the-date email with a photo of the two of you. Include essential information such as the date, city / area, your names and your telephone number so that your future guests can contact you (see Amrita and Joe's announcement in Chapter 2).

Opt for stationers who propose recycled paper products and vegetable-based inks. Some companies offer paper products that are not only compostable but also plantable. The paper, which is embedded with seeds, will turn into flowers, plants or herbs when placed in the ground. Reduce invitation inserts by communicating all those extra little details so essential for out-of-town guests and multi-day events by email or via a wedding website.

TROUSSEAU TEA

The trousseau tea is an afternoon party usually hosted by the mother of the bride – or the groom! – with family, neighbours and colleagues who are not invited to the wedding. Although tradition has it that the mother of the bride lays out her daughter's trousseau, most of the tea party guests would be keener on a

---

4   What is a 'carbon imprint'? Sometimes referred to as a 'carbon footprint', it is a measure of how much more CO_2 a person uses than is replaced by natural processes or personal environmental action (see Resources).

short appearance by the future bride and groom. However you decide to handle it, the trousseau tea is a great way to include people from your extended circle.

WEDDING GARB
Bride
Who says the bride must wear an outrageously expensive white wedding robe? Even if you are offered a family heirloom dress, choose a dress style and colour that makes you look good and will feel comfortable (including the shoes!) throughout the day's festivities. Then there's the weather. At most weddings, the groom swelters in his rented suit and the bride wishes for a dress with long sleeves or at least an elegant wrap.

Bridegroom
Why can't the bridegroom bend the rules too? An Indian groom broke (Western) tradition by wearing his family's traditional kurta set. Another wore a kilt made with his family's dress tartan. (*Hint:* If you've never sported a kurta or a kilt in public, wear it around town for a few days before the wedding.) Choosing comfortable footwear applies to the groom too.

Bridesmen and groomsladies?
Rare is the couple with attendants who all look great in the same matching dress or suit. In some cultures, this fact is less important than having them wear identical wedding garb. If you can get away with it, let your wedding party choose what they want to wear from clothes they already own or can rent. Specify a theme or style for women's dresses, such as length or colour. Men may be asked to avoid ties with patterns and stripes – or on the contrary, have them wear the same bowler hat, shades or pink and red striped socks as the groom! The

diversity of their clothing can add to rather than detract from the beauty of your wedding photos.

PHOTOS AND PHOTOGRAPHERS

Of course you want great wedding pictures! What kind? Documentary photos are candid or spontaneous. They tell the story of your wedding day. Portraiture photography produces posed pictures of the two of you, your friends and family in front of various backdrops. Artistic tends toward capturing spontaneous fun moments. Editorial wedding photography is about making a statement. Whichever kind or mix of styles you choose, identify the key people and emotions you want the photographer to capture.

Since you'll be spending most of the day with your photographer it is important to choose someone whose personality you like, and to feel that your vision of the event is shared. The photographer should be attentive and respectful of you, your celebrant, the musicians and your guests. A wedding photographer blends in with the guests (no war correspondent gear) and moves about discreetly. A true professional gets great shots without ever annoying the professionals by entering their space, or irritating your mother-in-law by blocking her view.

BEST WISHES

Think of the birds' health and replace the rice traditionally thrown at weddings with birdseed or, depending on your venue, wildflower seeds. Use bubbles made of liquid soap. Even adults enjoy blowing soap bubbles; they make for lovely end-of-ceremony photos.

Balloon launches are popular but not appreciated by fauna or flora. Two types of balloons are widely in use: latex and Mylar. Neither should be filled with helium and launched on account of the risks to the environment. Mylar nylon balloons are often coated with a metallic finish; they are not classified as biodegradable and do not decompose. Latex (natural rubber) takes about six months to decompose. Fish, fowl and other animals may die if they ingest bits or get caught in the strings tied to balloons. Latex balloons can be blown up the old-fashioned way, used in a controlled setting and then composted.

TRAVEL

What unique wedding transportation exists in your area? If your wedding is near a body of water, the bride may make her entrance from a boat. Or the two of you may leave your ceremony in a kayak or a canoe. One bride arrived on a donkey, another on a Vespa. A Dutch groom had his bride hop on the back of his bicycle, and then pedalled her across the street to their reception venue.

Reduce the distance your guests will need to go in motor vehicles. Choose venues for the wedding ceremony and reception that are nearby. One couple hired a bus to bring their out-of-town guests from the hotel to the wedding venue and back again. Guests at a wedding in a mountain lodge arrived in ski lifts. No one had to worry about finding the venue, about getting lost on unfamiliar roads in the dark or about drinking and driving after the festivities.

COCKTAIL AND TABLEWARE

If you serve an unusual dish or drink at your cocktail or reception, take the time to explain its significance to your guests. Consider the ecological impact of plastic decorations, cups, plates and cutlery and compare that against the price of renting some of these items. If you decide to go for disposable, suitable solutions do exist such as compostable, recyclable, biodegradable tableware (made of bamboo) and compostable cocktail and dinner napkins free of dyes, inks and fragrances made of paper recycled without chlorine bleach. Wrap your leftover cheese, cake and even salads in non-plastic wraps made of unbleached cloths of varying sizes, coated in beeswax and jojoba oil (such as Abeego). There are also eco-friendly alternatives to trash bags.

FLOWERS

No one says that a bride must carry flowers. If you do want flowers, choose locally grown blooms that are in season. An eco-friendly option is potted flowers, plants or topiaries which can double as table decorations – and then be recycled one more time as thank-you gifts for your wedding party. Blooms are natural but not necessarily organic or eco-friendly. Many plants are boosted with chemicals, grown under harsh working conditions or, if out of season where you live, must be flown in from across the world.

A couple who married in an old pump house decorated it with tea candles in glass yoghurt pots and garden flowers. Guests carried these items to the nearby reception venue and placed them on each table. Joe and Amrita's favourite books, placed at the centre of each table, along with a framed quote and a single flower, doubled as table themes and decorations. Other newlyweds chose to group their guests by tables named for a destination that had a special place in the couple's life together. Each guest received an 'airline ticket' for a destination / table.

THE FIRST BOTTOMLINE

An informal study that attempted to calculate the ratio of wedding costs to salary revealed that Americans spend 15–100 per cent of their yearly salary on their wedding (Weddingbee 2010). This data is a benchmark, not an expectation. Your budget should be aligned with your joint income, values, priorities and goals for your future together. It makes no sense to bow to pressure from relatives, friends, social media – or spending reports.[5]

Think carefully about *how* your values are reflected in your choices and goals for the event.

CUT DOWN THE GUEST LIST?!

Consider having two – or even three – guest lists: one for the ceremony and cocktail and another for the ceremony, cocktail and reception. The first list includes people you feel obliged to invite such as your father's boss. If you go this route use two separate venues or figure in ample time between the two phases of your event. Organizing a trousseau tea is a third way to include people in the celebration who do not figure in your inner circle (see *tool Prioritizing*).

Venues

The ceremony venue and the reception are often the most costly items in the wedding budget. Even top venues usually have lower rates for certain dates and periods of the year. Consider marrying on an ordinary weekday (rather than Saturday or a holiday) between November and April (except December) at a venue that works for both the ceremony and the reception.

Celebrant / presider

A truly professional celebrant sets their rates carefully. Most online wedding calculators estimate $300 (approx. £225) for the person who presides the ceremony. While this represents a generous 'tip' for a salaried religious leader or civil officiant, it constitutes a very low fee for a professional celebrant, who

5   The national average cost of a wedding in the United States in 2016 hit $35,329, not including the honeymoon (Knot 2016) while the median household income that year was $57,617 (United States Census Bureau 2017). Couples can often count on contributions from family or other sources to foot the bill. On average couples now pay 8 per cent less of their wedding costs than ten years ago: 2017 data (2007 data) 36% (44%) couple, 36% (46%) parents and 28% (10%) 'other sources' (WeddingWire 2017).

spends anywhere from 20 to 40 hours helping you create and then presiding over your custom ceremony. The celebrant's fee is usually more than that of the videographer but less than the florist, the photographer or the wedding planner. One way of cutting down costs is to prepare your ceremony with the celebrant and ask a reliable discreet friend or relative to preside. On the other hand, a professional celebrant makes the services of a wedding planner at the ceremony redundant.

Vendors

If you find it necessary to negotiate with vendors, do it carefully and respectfully. There are ways to cut costs without insulting anyone or foregoing their services. In the case of the photographer, for example, you can reduce the fee by cutting down the number of hours and photos. Ask your photographer to arrive after you have dressed or to cover only the ceremony and the first part of the cocktail. Complete your wedding album with your friends' best photos of the event. You are unlikely to need a wedding planner if you hold your wedding in a hotel or other venue designed to receive wedding parties.

5

CREATING THE CEREMONY

'Let's take look at your Checklist and see where we are today. Then we'll make a timeline for what remains to be done,' proposes Terry, the celebrant Joe and Amrita hired to help them design their custom wedding ceremony. Six months before their wedding date the couple have nearly completed the planning phase and are well into the creating phase.

'We'll have a short ceremony with all our guests in the park on Saturday morning under a light canopy,' explains Joe. 'All the accoutrements must arrive with us and be taken away when we leave the ceremonial space. Our brunch will be held a few hundred yards away in the terrace area around the SeaGlass Carousel. I'm sure the children will love riding those iridescent fish as much as we do! The reception venue is settled now too: on Saturday evening we'll celebrate with close friends and family at the Morgan Library.'

Amrita adds, 'Tyler's now got his licence as a Marriage Officiant from the City Clerk's Office. Our invitations go out next week.' Taking out a notebook marked 'ceremony', she continues: 'Last week we sent you three keywords: Respect, Generosity, Friendship and an early version of our vow.'

'After taking another look at the diagram of our relationship, we made a few minor changes,' Joe explains. 'Feeling safe in our relationship and eating with others are so important to us that we added "protect" and "nourish" to the list.' Amrita hands him a page from their notebook which he passes on to Terry. 'Here's the final version of our vow.'

'So, you've distilled your ideas down to five keywords,' observes Terry, 'which you've expressed simply and beautifully in this vow... Let's look now at the Coherence test and see how your keywords are conveyed in the decisions you made during the planning phase... I remember you wanted to include a wedding sari. Is this the "canopy" you referred to earlier?'

'That's right', replies Amrita. 'Before my grandmother died last year, she gave us her blessing. We'll suspend her wedding sari above our heads to "protect" us from direct sunlight and reduce shadows in our wedding photos. It feels like a good way to honour her.' 'At the end of the ceremony, Tyler will invite the guests to join us in "nourishing" brunch,' laughs Joe.

'What about other objects, texts or gestures that unpack these keywords for your guests?' asks Terry.

'Nelia will read this text we wrote about respect,' explains Amrita. 'When we showed it to her she pointed out that it was written from our perspective and wouldn't make sense to our guests. She helped us put it into third person. Here it is':

> The first gift Joe and Amrita exchanged was respect. They were raised very differently. Intuitively they realized early on that they could not take anything for granted. They determined to practise respect in their everyday conversations and acts.
>
> In Joe's work respect means listening carefully to other's ideas and being able to put aside petty disagreements. After a tough day, Joe used to just flop down on a soft chair and listen to music. He now appreciates coming home to Amrita's ritual of reviewing the day over drinks and nibbles.
>
> Libraries have many rules. Amrita sees respect as following rules that strengthen community – and questioning those that don't. Since silence is the rule that seems most difficult for people to respect in a library she tries to temper any reproaches at work, and at home, with kindness.
>
> Many of you travelled far to celebrate with them. Out of respect for you and all your different cultures and languages, Amrita and Joe chose a simple, natural setting they enjoy. They hope that you all feel comfortable here too. They want to thank their families and friends for their support and presence today. This sign of your respect for their choice in partners is the greatest gift you can offer them.

'Our friends Halvar and Filippa will read our text on "friendship". They *were in our first yoga class, so it will also be about how we met. We'll send it to you as soon as we can,' promises Amrita.*

'As for "generosity",' explains Joe, 'we've been exploring what evokes generous feelings for us. We've come up with trying out a new kind of coffee, a lazy weekend at home in pyjamas, reading our favourite books, a surprise bouquet of flowers, receiving a photo from an old friend, maple syrup brunches, combing a beach for sea glass, a ski weekend with friends, a text message that says "I'm thinking of you", a meal at a good Indian restaurant, a visit from a friend or family members...'

'You're doing really well,' Terry says. 'Your keywords are reflected in various ways throughout the ceremony. Use the tool for gestures and other objects. Keep up the good work! See you in two weeks!'

Joe & Amrita

Figure 5.1. Joe and Amrita's relationship
Joe is French-Canadian, raised in a culturally Christian family. He has never been married but has a seven-year-old daughter, Sarah, from a previous relationship. He works in social networking and loves to cook and sail. Amrita was born in the United States of Indian parents who divorced when she was young. She appreciates certain Hindu practices but does not consider herself religious. Amrita, a university librarian, reads mostly fiction, jogs regularly and enjoys monthly museum visits with her best friend Karen. Together the couple enjoy spending long hours over a meal, yoga, the zoo, travelling and time with their friends.

Although we have little explicit knowledge of how rituals were created by our ancestors, anthropologist Matthieu Smyth points out that ritualization was not always left to specialists (personal communication 2016). In early, less hierarchical cultures, hunter-gatherer groups shared ritualmaking or assumed it informally on an ad hoc basis. Just as hunter-gatherers could afford to choose their partners (see Chapter 1) they could also afford to create rituals to mark their unions.

Ethologist Ellen Dissanayake notes that what made ceremonial rituals prime opportunities for the arts in premodern societies remains true today. Special costumes, masks and other body ornamentation; altered and embellished artefacts and surroundings; chanting, dancing, singing, drumming, altered language and dramatic performances transform from ordinary to extraordinary bodies, objects, environments, movements and even utterances. This is what makes people remember, accept, internalize, or guide their lives by ceremonial rituals (Dissanayake 2017, pp.155, 159).

MAKING THE ORDINARY EXTRAORDINARY

'Doing something' to mark the important occasions in our lives comes naturally to us too. Artistic ritual addresses and satisfies our psychological needs as humans. The ceremonies we practise in times of uncertainty are essential to individual and collective welfare. They create and reinforce emotionally reassuring and psychologically necessary feelings of close relationship with others and of belonging to a group (Dissanayake, personal communication 2016).

The three phases presented in Part II – planning, creating and realizing – apply to all ritualization. It is worth reminding the reader here that our human need to mark a union can be met by ready-made or bespoke crafted rituals. Fiancés who celebrate with the rituals of religious or civic institutions are involved in the planning and realizing phases but need not bother with the middle phase: creating ritual. The institution has already done the work of interpreting the meaning and the ritual expression of the occasion for them. It also puts a professional at the couple's disposal to preside the traditional ready-to-celebrate rites.

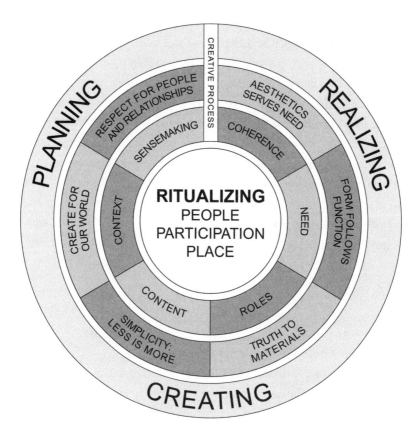

Figure 5.2. The creative process
This diagram, inspired by the Bauhaus movement, illustrates the creative process of ritualmaking in three phases: planning, creating and realizing (see the outer ring). Ritual design is based on a few simple principles. The essential ritual 'materials' are shown at the centre of the diagram: people, participation and place. Gestures, words and objects anchor the life event in reality. The innermost ring identifies the pillars of ritual design. The second ring presents rules for designing rituals (see the notes at the end of this chapter).

THE CREATIVE PROCESS

The creating phase of ritualmaking is what sets custom ceremonies apart from the ready-made ritual. The craft of ritual so familiar to the ancients depends on the intensely creative process employed by the artisan. Crafting effective new rituals that work requires a healthy imagination, respect for ritual materials, knowledge of ritual design and rigour (see Figure 5.2).

Cultural psychologist Luca Tateo describes this process as the amazing capacity of the human imagination to embody and produce abstract signs. Imagination involves an incessant shifting back and forth between thoughts or concepts and embodied gestures and objects.

Even more astonishing, the interplay between the individual and collective imagination allows human beings to enhance both self-regulation and social regulation (Tateo 2016, p.50).

Applying this process to the craft of ritual requires a safe setting and that the couple dedicate significant time and energy to exploring what the occasion means to them. Stephen Porges insists that feeling safe is the decisive factor for both our wellbeing and creative activity. 'What would it be like if creative people felt safe, or...more people could become creative if they felt safe?' he asks (Porges 2012, n.p.). The senses and sensemaking are inseparable components of this process. They lead the couple's exploration of the subtle boundaries of being human in the present, help them reframe the past and formulate their fears and dreams for the future. This is how we repackage ritual as alternative technology of the body–heart–mind. In a safe setting it can transform people and foster an organic communal body that enhances social, and even geopolitical, stability.

CREATING PHASE

During the planning phase you will have clarified who you are as a couple and your shared ritual profile (see *Questionnaire on my ritual profile* and *Inventory on ritual profile for weddings*). In this phase you will identify your joint values and common goals.

The most touching and sincere custom ceremonies are composed of original work. Creating material for your wedding that makes sense means calling on the artist in you. You do not need stock vows or to scour the internet for overused texts that express others' views of their love and marriage. In the same way, your friends and families' views on these subjects are great for the wedding reception but inappropriate at your ceremony. Of course, you are free to check out what others believe coupleship means to them and to listen to what your entourage thinks should be important to you. Even so – as a favour to yourselves – do so only *after* you have identified your keywords and written at least the first draft of your vow. In most cases, you will be surprised and pleased with what you have done.

Use the tools at the end of this chapter to identify the personal experiences, cultural traditions, stories and objects that make sense to you in this context. Let them point you in the right direction as you delve deeply into your relationship asking yourselves questions such as: *Why and how* are we ritualizing (see tool with this name)? What is at the heart of the ceremony (see tools *Core values* and *Keywords*)?

Contemporary secular ritual is designed around the couple's joint values and relationship. Joe and Amrita started out by drawing a diagram of their relationship (see Figure 5.1). They found that visualizing who they are separately first made it easier for them to concentrate on their joint concerns.

CONTENT

Your wedding vow is the highpoint of your ceremony and the first element you craft. It evolves instinctively out of your values and keywords. Your keywords also influence your choice of music, symbolic objects and gestures as well as the texts you write for the ceremony.

Primal ritual materials for your ceremony include people, participation and place (see centre of Figure 5.2). From these three sources come the content of the ceremony, the words, gestures and objects that anchor wedding rituals in the couple's reality. The content of your ceremony is centred round your keywords or values and ripples out from there. Let your interests and values inspire you as you determine which words, music and gestures to use, then check to be sure they are coherent with your values (see *Coherence test*).

Content

- Keywords
- Vow
- Texts (expression of keywords, welcome, closing)
- Gestures & symbols (decorations)
- Music

Format

- Beginning (entry, welcome)
- Middle (vow, texts, gestures, symbols)
- End (closing, exit)

Figure 5.3. Two inboxes

FORMAT

All ceremonies have a beginning, a middle and an end. The format or order of your ceremony represents the framework for your content. Once you have determined what is at the heart of your ceremony and the content has been created, take stock of your different elements. When you see that you have all the elements together, put them in the order that makes the most sense to you.

Since the DJ, musicians and readers need to be able to consult this information at a glance, fit the synopsis on one single sheet of paper. Use this one-page outline to make a complete version that introduces the elements of the ceremony. Like a libretto, this full version should contain all the words and gestures, plus the stage directions (who does what, when, where and how). See the tool *Format of the ceremony* in this chapter.

TIMING

Build in time during this phase to let your ideas settle. Imagine performing your rituals and how they will feel to you on the day of your wedding. Couples who have reserved their venue a year in advance are encouraged to visit on the day and hour they have planned for their ceremony. Take pictures of the room or garden so that you can remember the layout and how the light shines at that time of day.

Once you are satisfied with your format, test it out in situ. The ceremony becomes more concrete when you go through the choreography in the setting you have chosen. Walk it through a few times, alone with your presider (without parents, photographer and friends). Even if you are nervous on the day of the wedding your feet will 'remember' where to take you during the ceremony.

Finally, draw up reminder lists that take into account the transition to social gathering.

PAUSE

RISK FACTORS FOR THE CREATING PHASE

It is ever so tempting to buy a pile of books or to spend hours on the internet picking things out of others' ceremonies. Trust yourself! Check out how others went about it after you have decided what you want to write or do. Most people find their choices confirmed. Surprises, including improvised contributions, confuse and overwhelm people. They are welcome at the reception but not appropriate for the ceremony.

Grimes: Ritualizing with our own stuff

Some rituals are not much more than sugary confections, all tantalization and immediate gratification, but ultimately leaving us starved for real meaning. Pilfering other people's rituals can turn into a spiritual imperialism that mirrors Western culture's historic sense of ownership of the world. One of the reasons we might become interested in the rituals of hunter-gatherer societies is because we are moving around a lot, like hunters and gatherers. But our sense of connection with space and our sense of loyalty to a particular place have changed; our ritual sensibility has changed as well.

Like traditional rituals, do-it-yourself (DIY) ritual can result in complicity, empty gestures, people having to do something they resist doing. In either case, deep-seated resentment can lie under the surface of ritual acts. If DIY rituals are really going to meet our needs, they have to be made up of the familiar, not the exotic: metaphors that make sense to us, language that reflects the way we see the world and symbols with which we have a history. Start with your own broken teacups, the stuff in your backyard, keepsakes in the backs of drawers. Begin there, not with someone else's rituals. (R.L. Grimes, personal communication 2016)

TOOLBOX

TOOLS FOR THE CREATING PHASE

The toolbox contains basic tools for the creating phase of crafting wedding rituals.

The two of you form the crafting team for your unique wedding ceremony. The tools here provide you with the means to complete the creating phase of the checklist. Let them guide you as you identify the context and create the content of your ceremony, assign roles and figure out how it all fits together (see also *Ritual design* at the end of this chapter).

Remember to take a short break after each exercise.

Why and how?

How do you imagine your ceremony? Without realizing it, most couples have rather clear ideas of what their ceremony should be like. They can often describe all or parts of it as though they were watching it on film. The challenge is to bring the partner's ideas together into one film, and then to share it with the person who presides their ceremony. This exercise serves as a base for your discussions and facilitates brainstorming on what you want for your ceremony.

Set aside about 15–30 minutes for the exercise: 5–10 minutes for the first part and 10–20 minutes for the second and third set of questions. Follow your gut feelings. Note down the answers that come readily.

Materials needed

A sheet of paper and writing tools for each of you, plus one extra sheet for your joint vision of the ceremony. Try using different coloured sheets for your separate and joint responses.

Questions

First of all, work separately on the questions below.

- Why is this occasion important to me (need)?

- Why do I want to have the ceremony here and now (context)?

- What do I want our wedding to convey (sensemaking)? (e.g. our respect for each other, our dreams for the future...)

- What do I NOT want to see, hear or do (content)?

- Briefly, how do I envisage the ceremony (roles)?

  ◦ How do I imagine our role? (Will I arrive at the ceremonial space alone or together with my partner? How will I stand to say our vow? How do I imagine the end of our ceremony?)

  ◦ What is the role of our presider and the participants? (Where will they sit and stand?)

- How do I want to feel at the end of the ceremony (coherence)?

Second, set aside judgement and take turns sharing your ideas about the ceremony. Again, trust your feelings and the answers that come easily.

On a fresh page, note your joint answers to these questions.

- Why is this occasion important to us (need)?

- Why did we choose to have the ceremony here and now (context)?

- What do we want our wedding to convey (sensemaking)? (e.g. our respect for each other, our dreams for the future…)

- What do we NOT want to see, hear or do (content)?

- Briefly, how do we envisage the ceremony (roles)?

  ◦ How do we imagine our role? (Will we arrive at the ceremonial space alone or together?)

  ◦ How will we stand to say our vow? How do we imagine the end of our ceremony?)

  ◦ What is the role of our presider and the participants? (Where will they sit and stand?)

- How do we want to feel at the end of the ceremony (coherence)?

- How do we want our guests to feel at the end of our ceremony?

Finally, tackle the areas that need to be clarified or negotiated. Now make a final version of this third document. If you are not agreed on all aspects, note the differences and keep these issues in mind. The reasons – and solutions – may well come to you as you move on through the next tasks.

 ### Core values

This tool is designed to help you identify the pillars of your life and relationship. It looks at how values evolve over time (see suggestions for terms in Table 5.1). Your work on this exercise is central to the creation process.

Variant: Instead of words think of positive images, concepts or themes that evoke what is at the heart of your relationship.

First round – my values

Separately, answer the first and second groups of questions (past, present).

Past: values I grew up with

- What was I taught to value?

- What was I taught about the importance of

    ◦ achievement/success

    ◦ work at school/job

    ◦ money/power

    ◦ relationships with others

    ◦ appearance

    ◦ independence

    ◦ hobbies, sports and other free-time activities

    ◦ sexuality

    ◦ religion/spiritual practice

    ◦ nature/the environment.

Present: values I cherish now

- Which of the above values have I discarded or adapted to my life today?

- Which values have I retained?

- What set of core values are important to me now?

Refine your list until you have a maximum of 10 words.

Second round – my view of our values

Separately, make a list of the values you see as being important to your relationship.

- Which of your individual values have you integrated in your life with your partner?

- Which core values did you identify as being important for your relationship today?

Third round – values we both cherish

Together, exchange and compare the lists you made in the second round. Frequently, partners will use different words to identify the same concepts. Look behind the words or phrases you and your partner have chosen to see where your values are similar and where they are different.

Make a joint list.

- Which words in this new list best fit your shared definition of love? e.g. For us, love means… OR Love is not complete without… OR These words represent the foundation or the pillars of our love: …

Hone your list down to a maximum of 10 core values. Now you are ready to see how these words or concepts can be used in your ceremony.

The values (words) in Table 5.1 are to be used with the tools *Core values* and *Keywords*.

TABLE 5.1. TERMS EXPRESSING CORE VALUES

Accepting	Accommodating	Accurate	Adventurous
Affectionate	Agreeable	Allegiance	Altruistic
Ambitious	Analytical	Appreciative	Articulate
Artistic	Assertive	Attentive	Authentic
Balance	Beauty	Broad-minded	Calm
Candid	Care	Caution	Cheerful
Comforting	Committed	Communication	Compassion
Cooperative	Courageous	Courteous	Creative
Cultivated	Curiosity	Decisive	Dependable
Devoted	Dignity	Diplomatic	Discreet
Easy-going	Educated	Effective	Efficient
Elegance	Empathy	Encouraging	Entertaining
Enthusiastic	Excellence	Exploration	Fair
Family	Fidelity	Flexibility	Forgiving

cont.

Forthright	Freedom	Friendship	Frugal
Gentle	Good sport	Happiness	Hard-working
Gracious	Grateful	Generous	Genuine
Harmony	Helpful	Honest	Honourable
Hopeful	Humane	Humble	Humour
Imaginative	Industrious	Inquisitive	Insightful
Integrity	Intelligence	Intuitive	Joy
Justice	Kindness	Knowledge	Leadership
Learning	Loyalty	Maturity	Mindfulness
Modesty	Motivated	Nature	Open-minded
Passion	Peace	Perceptive	Perfection
Piety	Pleasant	Pleasure	Polite
Power	Practical	Pragmatic	Precision
Prudence	Purity	Quick-witted	Realism
Relaxation	Reliability	Resourceful	Respectful
Security	Self-control	Self-discipline	Selflessness
Serenity	Service	Sharing	Simplicity
Sincerity	Skilfulness	Sociable	Solidarity
Spirited	Spirituality	Stability	Strength
Support	Sympathy	Tactful	Talented
Teamwork	Thoughtful	Tidy	Togetherness
Tolerant	Optimistic	Orderly	Originality
Truthful	Trust	Understanding	Unity
Valour	Well-mannered	Well-spoken	Wisdom

 Two inboxes

The creative process of ritual design involves two parallel activities: making and gathering appropriate materials and putting these elements in to a particular order. The content and the format of the ceremony must serve your ritual strategy.

Create two folders to which you both have access (e.g. Dropbox, Evernote). Label one 'content' and the other 'format'. Add subfolders to each of these main folders that correspond to the different aspects of the ceremony, e.g. texts, gestures, symbols, decorations, etc. You are both responsible for adding content and modifying the order of your ceremony.

Keywords

Instead of following the crowd with a wedding ceremony about 'love' and 'marriage', you now have the means to take the creative process to new heights with your own definition of what these words mean to you as a couple.

In the same way that rose oil is the essence of a rose, you will identify keywords or phrases that represent the quintessence of your relationship. Take out your joint list of core values. The goal this time around is to distil the list to three to five keywords or short phrases.

Testing your short list

- Do these words or phrases guide how we conduct our relationship now?

- Skip ahead in time and imagine your life together in 5, 10 and then 15 years. Will these values guide us in the future too?

Your keywords and the values they represent undergird all your choices for your wedding, from the invitation and venue to your vows, the texts you write, the music you play and the gestures you perform at your ceremony.

NB It is easier for you to build your ceremony around simple words or phrases – and for your guests to retain them.

Composing your vow

There is no wedding without a ceremony and no ceremony without a wedding vow. Everything else – from music to wedding garb to the cake – serves to highlight the couple's public commitment. Guests are often surprised to learn that their duty goes beyond their presence and a present. As witnesses of the vow, they have a responsibility to help the couple keep whatever it is they promise.

As we saw in Chapter 2, many new models of coupleship are in vogue. Few women today promise fidelity in exchange for payment of their credit card bill. In this day and age, an egalitarian vow makes the most sense. Many couples confuse declarations of love with their vow. A vow expresses what love and commitment mean to you. A vow is a pledge or contract with your beloved. This promise implies a solemn moment that is often preceded by both a formal declaration of intent and a public declaration of love.

Declaration of intent

The vow is often proceeded by what is known as a 'declaration of intent' which may be a simple statement or take a question/answer format.

Statement: It is my intention, [Name], to marry you/take you as my partner in our lifelong journey together.

Question/answer: [Name], is it your intention to take [Name of partner] as your [wife, husband, partner...]?

Declaration of love

It is inadvisable to improvise this short personal text about what your partner means to you. I ask the partners to send me their texts shortly after they write their joint vow. If they want it to be a surprise but one or the other shows concern about the content, I'll let them know if there is great disparity in the length or tone of the declaration.

Do you need inspiration for a public declaration of your love? What do you appreciate about your partner? List three to five things you appreciate about her/him. What first attracted you to your partner? When were you sure you wanted to stay with her/him? Recount the moment or event that you convinced you s/he was the right partner for you. Or, if you feel truly creative, write a rhyming poem or make an acrostic of your beloved's name.

The vow

Your keywords are really all you need to compose a meaningful wedding vow. Although it is no easier to keep short vows than long ones, a concise vow is definitely easier to remember, even years later. The most touching promises are simple and sincere. Your joint vow should be written and pronounced in the first person singular: I promise (or 'will' or 'pledge') ... The keywords that appear (in italic) in each of the following examples should be replaced with your own keywords. Modify the formulas with phrases that feel right to you.

Your promise may be straightforward:

My love [or Name], I promise to nourish our love/marriage/relationship through *honesty*, *respect*, *kindness* and *loyalty*.

Somewhat more complex:

My love [or Name], I promise be *honest* with you, to show you *kindness* and to share your joys and sorrows. As co-caretaker of our relationship I promise to nurture it with *loyalty* and *respect*. As your friend and lover, I promise to do all I can to make our dreams come true.

Or even elaborate:

My love [or Name],

From this day forward, I pledge you *respect*, *loyalty*, *honesty* and *kindness*. Hand in hand, heart to heart, I take you, my destined mate, above all others, without reservation.

Compose one or two drafts, then set the vow aside for a week or two. Set a date for discussing it with your celebrant. When you come back to the vow you may well find that it only needs a tweak or two.

Before the big day, make sure you practise your personal text and your vow. Use the suggestions in *Guidelines for readers* to feel at ease speaking before your guests. If you decide to commit your texts to memory make sure the presider has a final copy, just in case you need prompting.

Now you are ready to unpack your keywords in the elements that build up to the moment you pronounce your vow.

Plumbing the meaning

Now that your vow is written you are ready to take sensemaking and creativity to yet another level. Just as your keywords form the base of your promise they are also central to the rest of the content of your ceremony. This is the first of several tools that focus on the creation of original material for the buildup to your vow such as the texts read, your choice of music, symbols and gestures (see the tools below).

Your keywords represent distilled values that will help you plumb the complexities of your relationship. Take the icon for this tool as an example of how to explore the meaning of an image or word. The technical sense of 'plumb' refers to measuring the quality or state of being true or authentic. A plumbline is a noun; the word 'plumb', which can be a noun, a verb, an adverb or an adjective, has several meanings:

Technical sense: A plumbline is a tool that consists of a small, heavy object (sometimes called a 'bob') attached to a string or rope. It is used to see if something (such as a wall) is perfectly vertical or plumb (noun). It is used to ensure a wall or chimney is plumb, that is, not leaning to one side (adjective). Plumb also means exactly straight down or up: in a perfectly vertical position (adverb).

Literary sense: Plumb refers to how we examine (something) in a careful and complete way in order to understand it (verb).

Materials needed

A sheet of paper or two for each word and writing and drawing tools.

Plumbing words

Place the word at the centre of the page. Note around it what comes up for the two of you as you explore the word from different vantage points. You may prefer to begin with logical definitions or from other angles such as how the word touches your senses, what emotions it brings up and what experiences the word evokes in you. If you are proficient in mind-mapping feel free to use it to plumb the meaning of your keywords.

Dictionary definitions

Each word you have chosen has a dictionary definition and subjective meanings. Couples with a methodical approach may start – as we did above with 'plumb' – by looking up the dictionary definition. If you speak several languages, see how your words translate, or if they get lost in translation.

Senses

What senses are awakened in you by this word? How does it make you feel? Relaxed or rejuvenated? Where do you feel 'kindness', for example, in your body? Is it warm or cool? Does it have a colour or a texture? What sights, sounds, tastes or smells does the word bring to mind? Does the word make you feel elevated or grounded? Sad, pensive or joyous? Note these reactions on the corresponding page.

Resonance

Another port of entry is resonance, that is the associations or strong emotions, these words stir up. Let's say you chose the words beauty – generosity – security. While one person may hold beauty as an aesthetic sense, another may think of physical attractiveness and another the feeling s/he gets while looking at a sunset. Generosity can bring up the rich feeling of giving for some and evoke receiving for others. Security may mean money in the bank for one person, strong locks on windows and doors for another and feeling safe and cosy under a warm blanket on a stormy night for yet another.

Experiences

Perhaps the words remind you of lyrics from a song you heard the day you met. Maybe there is a poem, a story or a quote that highlights your relationship. Perhaps a sculpture, a piece of art or a film reminds you of special times together. Note these ideas next to the corresponding keyword.

Once you have a few connections that tie each word with feelings, memories and experiences that are important for both of you, move on to *Writing a meaningful text.*

Writing a meaningful text

Compile one or two of the best strong expressions or experiences related to each word. Then turn these situations into a short story or vignette that reveals, concretely, how this value is or has been put into practice in your life and relationship. Aim for a minimum of three and a maximum of seven texts.

A word of encouragement

The writings of great authors, philosophers and other wise folks may seem like a hard act to follow. Yet I have seen even close family and friends zone out during readings of borrowed writing. You may worry that your guests will find what you write too simple, too homey... Don't let this discourage you. Those who dare to write their own texts soon find that it is easier than they imagined – and that the words are likely to touch guests more deeply than any borrowed text ever could. Less is more; a simple account based on your life is indeed the ultimate sophistication (see *Notes on Ritual Design* at the end of this chapter).

Example 1

If one of your keywords is 'tenderness' and Elvis Presley was crooning 'Love Me Tender' on the car radio the day you decided to live together, you've got the subject for one vignette. You also remember a funny story about getting how you cajoled her in to giving you a little TLC for a sprained ankle... So, now you have two and you may have to choose between these situations.

Example 2

Another keyword is 'peaceful'. One of your most memorable holidays together is a kayak trip around the islands off the coast of Vancouver. The weather was cool, the air crisp and the sky clear. As you paddled to your campsite, the setting sun reflected off the still water of a small bay... Describe not only what you saw but also the wild birds you heard, the scratchy wool sweater you pulled on and the smell of cooking on an open fire.

Example 3

You want to emphasize 'compassion'. As you queue up at a checkout, someone cuts in front of you. Instead of getting angry, your partner remarks matter-of-factly: 'You must be in a hurry.' The woman glances at him and bursts into tears: 'I'm sorry, I did not see you. My dog just died. He's in the trunk of my car. I'm buying a shovel but I'm not sure I even know how to use it...can you help me?'

Determine your point of view

Any piece of writing can be written from multiple points of view. In most cases, the vignette will be read at your wedding by a friend or family member. This means you should use the third person singular and plural (s/he/they) point of view for telling your story. If you decide to read the account yourselves, use first person singular and plural (I/we).

Build a series of short phrases

Feel free to use humour and your own expressions in your stories and anecdotes.

Repeat the process by writing one text for each keyword. Let the texts sit for a few hours, days or even weeks. Come back to them now and again to ask: Does this fit? Does it feel right? Make revisions as needed. Authenticity and coherence are of the essence.

Words of caution

Borrowing inspiring texts to help you unpack your keywords is also an option. Just as guests sit up to catch every word of a personal narrative, they will also tend their ear to listen to an original take on a well-known text. Again, rather than going for texts on 'love' and 'marriage', ferret out writing that expresses what these words mean to you. Feel free to adapt the text to your situation, or write your own take on the theme. Give credit where credit is due.

If you do decide to use a text as is, read it aloud a few times to make sure the language is accessible. Antiquated terms can roll off the tongue nicely, or not.

Make sure you understand the meaning, and the context, of any borrowed text you use. Edgar Allan Poe's *Annabel Lee* and Elizabeth Barrett Browning's popular *Sonnet 43*, better known as 'How Do I Love Thee?' both refer to the romantic power of love...in death.

Remember that your guests' attention spans are limited, especially during an outdoor wedding. Keep it short and sweet.

As for texts written for you by friends, save them for the reception. Remember the ceremony is your showcase. Your loved ones need to hear about what this occasion means to you with your own words. You have their full attention for 20–30 minutes. It may be the only chance you ever get to tell them what you expect of yourselves and of them. Use this time well!

♫ Just the right music

Music is not obligatory for a wedding, but it is a great way to create a romantic atmosphere and to support strong emotions. Whether you choose the latest hit tunes or traditional wedding pieces, all of the music in your ceremony should enhance the meaning the occasion has for you and reinforce your ritual strategy.

Frequently asked questions

Shall we hire musicians or play recorded music?

How the music is relayed depends on your priorities and budget. Hiring live musicians comes at a price, but it has many advantages. Musicians add to the festive atmosphere and reduce stress for guests, presider and newlyweds alike. Professional musicians can improvise with the presider to cover up unexpected events such as a late bride or the inevitable quack in planning. Participants accompanied by soft music feel more confident as they walk forward to read their text.

Whether the musicians are amateurs or professionals, make sure they can play the pieces you want to hear. Find out whether they play acoustic music or if they will need special equipment (like electricity). The presider should welcome them, show them where to set up and brief them on the order of the ceremony. If you opt for recorded music make sure someone, other than the presider, is responsible for putting it on at the right time. In both cases, the presider gives the cues to play.

How much music do we need?

You need at least two pieces of music, one for entering and one for exiting the ceremonial space. Fiancés who enter the ceremonial space separately often each choose a piece that fits their separate interests, culture or personality. Those who walk in together may opt for a reminder of a particular moment in their life together. Playing the right piece of music during the ceremony can reinforce your themes, or serve as a breather after an intensely emotional moment. Joyful music is great for the exit since it launches the social part of the wedding.

How long should the music be?

Timing is everything. The music you select for your entrance and exit must be long enough for you to move from one spot to another but not too long. You do not want your guests to become impatient for the ceremony or the festivities to begin. Nor do you do not want to have to walk the last 100 metres in total silence. Walk it through with the presider to estimate the length you need to respect your timing. Long pieces should be cropped or shortened by gently turning the sound down. Even a piece that is 2–3 minutes too long can seem out of place to a couple eager to pronounce their vows – as well as to guests sitting in the sun and young children.

Small gestures, big impact

Every culture uses gestures and symbols to mark important occasions. The rituals performed at a wedding must connect with the physical realities and spiritual needs of the couple and their entourage. Wearing new or special clothing, exchanging property (e.g. wedding rings) and sharing food and drink (social gathering) are widely understood aspects of the wedding ritual that fit secular settings. Art-filled expressions, such as a special arranged stage, dancing, singing or dramatic performances, transform ordinary bodies, objects, environments, movements and utterances into extraordinary ones that help people remember, accept, internalize or guide their lives.[1]

---

1   Cultural psychologist Luca Tateo explains this in terms of what he calls 'affective logic': 'the two statements "I am faithful to my spouse THEREFORE I wear the wedding ring" and "I wear the wedding ring THEREFORE I am faithful to my spouse" are equally valid. Affective logic is based on imaginative processes, and the relationship acquires value with respect to the person's continuous striving for "what's next"' (Tateo 2018, p.9).

Questions for the couple

- What do we need to do to feel like we have made the transition into married life?

- What symbolizes for us this new phase in our life?

- What do we want a gesture, symbol, dance or singing to express? Our union? Our future together? Appreciation for our parents? Gratitude to our friends?

- Is there something we feel we need to welcome or let go of?

- How can we use the symbols or gestures that are important to us to communicate our values?

Be curious

Investigate the gestures and symbols of your cultural tradition(s) or origin(s). Ask married relatives how they, and their parents, celebrated their marriage. At which point did your mother or grandmother feel married? One woman recounted feeling like a wife when her husband publicly carried her over the threshold of their new home. Maybe stomping on a glass at the end of your wedding ceremony is not your thing, but the gesture may inspire you to do something else that ties in with your core values and makes you feel married.

Symbols of the relationship

A couple of scientists subtly brought the symbol of the circle into their wedding. The first thing their guests saw was the circular ceremonial space, delineated from the rest of the garden by cross-sections of tree trunks. The welcoming words confirmed the place of their families and friends in the couple's inner circle. Their best man, a mathematician like the bride, read a text about this series of points aligned in perfect symmetry. The circumference divided by a circle's diameter yields Pi, a mysterious number that exemplifies infinity and irrationality. The newlyweds sealed their promise with a silent exchange of rings. The ceremony ended with a circle dance around the couple.[2] Throughout the years the golden circles on their fingers remind them of their vow to work for harmony as well as the mystery, irrationality and boundless character of love.

Objects in your closets

In preparation for the arrival of their first child, a couple who had been living together for 10 years found themselves moving house while organizing their wedding. As they sorted through their belongings and packed up boxes, they came across representations of the four seasons, all of a well-known site near their new home. An ink drawing of a Maypole dance symbolized springtime. Lightly clad people were featured on a postcard of a summer picnic. An old photo emphasized the saturated colours of autumn leaves and an oil painting captured the joy of red-cheeked children sledding down a hill. They blew three of the images up to poster size and gave the painting a new frame. Then they sat down to write two short texts recounting the spring and summer of their romance and two more outlining their hopes and dreams for the remaining seasons of their love.

Involve your guests

Simple, intentional acts, such as singing or dancing together, shaking hands or hugging, writing a thoughtful note in the guest book, making a speech at the reception, reinforce meaning and social ties during the wedding.

Warning

Avoid using a symbol or gesture just because you think you need one. An act closely associated with a religious rite cannot be used with impunity.[3] Be wary, too, of blindly appropriating gestures some authority claims belong to your culture, such as handfasting or smudging for North Americans

---

2   In contrast to the conservative nature of folk dance, informal circle dances serve the dancers by providing a supportive, safe environment for a physical, emotional and spiritual experience.

3   Is a religious figure expected to perform, witness or validate this gesture? This is a litmus test for the use of religious ritual in a secular ceremony. The same applies to lifting phrases such as 'I pronounce you...' from a civil ceremony. This official declaration, which follows the phrase: 'by the power invested in me by the state of...', is clearly reserved for civil officiants or celebrants who do in fact represent the state.

and 'cutting wood' for Europeans. Think twice about pilfering rituals from other cultures (see *Grimes: Ritualizing with our own stuff*). Practised outside their true context, these 'traditional' rites are often ambiguous, misleading or even alienating. In the same way, 'new' rituals such as mixing two kinds of earth, releasing butterflies or planting cut sunflower stalks in a pot of dirt can feel contrived, ethereal or foolish. Guests may well wonder about the significance of the cut log and sunflower stalks – and of what will become of them after the ceremony.

Format of the ceremony

The format of your ceremony is the framework that holds it together. Depending on the context, your format may be simple or involve an elaborate protocol (as for a televised wedding ceremony). Both of you should participate in the three rounds described below.

Sample order of a wedding ceremony

Entrance music – guests gather for the ceremony; participants and parents enter the ceremonial space; the couple enter, separately or together

Welcome – presider

Readings – friends and relatives (accompany readers with 30–60 seconds of live music)

Intention to marry

Declaration of love for partner

Joint vow

Sealing the vow – symbolic gesture: rings, kiss

Closing words – presider

Exit music – the couple guide guests from the ceremonial space to cocktail or reception

---

First round

Imagine who will do what and what will happen when, and what it will look like in the venue you have chosen. Play the 'film' in your head. Share and compare these ideas with your partner.

Second round

- Write up a simple order of events (see *Sample order of a wedding ceremony*); adapt it to meet your needs.

- Alternate lighter and more serious contributions. Prepare an introduction to each contribution that includes the name of the person who reads (text) or performs (music, dance) and their link to you.

- Sketch out the setting, measure the aisle and the distances.

- Mark out your ideal choreography.

- Include a seating plan with seats reserved in the front rows for immediate family members and your wedding party.[4]

- As you move through each aspect of the event, keep your core values in mind and check for coherence at each step (see *Coherence test*).

Third round

Visit the venue, if possible at the same hour of the day as the ceremony. With your 'Order of ceremony' in hand, walk it through to see if it works for you. Ask yourself: Do I feel comfortable standing here? Can I imagine standing or sitting here with family and friends in front of me? Do I feel all right having them that close/far away? Can I see the presider, musicians,

---

4   In some cultures, members of the wedding party are expected to precede the bride and groom into the ceremonial space and then to remain standing there for the duration of the ceremony. Those without training as professional soldiers find it difficult to be immobile for 30 minutes without scratching their noses or balancing from one foot to the other. Their presence is a challenge for choreography: where does one place the readers, the musicians, etc.? As well as for guests who try not to be distracted by them. Not to mention the photographer who must try to get a few good shots of the couple alone.

speakers? Do I feel comfortable with the choreography as a whole? If not, what can I change so as to feel more at ease?

Finalizing the order

Once you have determined the order, make a libretto version that contains all the words, plus the stage directions or choreography. Make a list of the items you will need at the venue on the day of the ceremony. Note who is responsible for bringing each one of them and for putting them into place.

Coherence test

The *Coherence test* ensures that the ceremony is consistent with your values and harmonious with the event as a whole. It should be used at several points during the creation process.

Once you have established your list of core values and keywords, use Table 5.2 to confirm the choices you made in the planning phase about Who, What, When and Where. Then let it help you assess your agreement about the date, your guest list and cost. As you move along in your planning, regularly compare your other choices with your core values.

Starting with your invitation, what makes it an appropriate invitation for our wedding? Is it the quality of the paper? The font and layout? How the invitation is worded?

In the same way, run through the entire ceremony, identifying where your values show through and where they do not.

- Do the choices we made in the planning phase regarding kind of ceremony, people, venue, date and time fit our core values? If so, we confirm them and move on. If not, how can we adapt them now to be more on target?

- How are our keywords expressed in each context? How might we communicate them more clearly in our ceremony?

- How does the ceremony fit in with our ritual strategy?

Use the grid in Table 5.2 to explore how you express your core values concretely in each phase of the creative process. Pencil your keywords in the top row and compare them with the different aspects of your preparation for the ceremony.

TABLE 5.2. COHERENCE GRID

🎚️ WEDDING ELEMENTS/CHOICES *(BELOW)*	OUR VALUES (KEYWORDS ACROSS)				
Invitation					
Ceremony venue					
Guest list					
Date / time					
Vow*					
Texts*					
Gestures*					
Symbols*					
Presider*					
Participation (friends and family)					
Cost					
Materials used (tables, chairs, serving)					
Decorations					
* see appropriate tool					

 NOTES ON RITUAL DESIGN

The Swiss architect Peter Zumthor is known for how he relentlessly exploits the sensory potential of materials in his work. Materials are crafted and joined to enhance experience of the world. He sees architecture as a form of resistance in a society that celebrates the inessential. For him, the physicality of materials puts us in contact with touch, smell and perhaps even the taste of the materials.

> The sense that I try to instil into materials is beyond all rules of composition, and their tangibility, smell, and acoustic qualities are merely elements of the language we are obliged to use. Sense emerges when I succeed in

bringing out the specific meanings of certain materials in my buildings, meanings that can only be perceived in just this way in this one building. (Zumthor 2006 [1998], p.10)

In Chapter 4 we explored how the main materials of ritualmaking – people, participation and place – fit into ritual strategy (see centre of Figure 5.2). Here we see how appropriate materials and design are essential for the success of architects, artisans and crafters of ritual alike.

PILLARS OF RITUAL DESIGN

The six pillars of ritual design are need, context, roles, content, sensemaking and coherence (see first circle in Figure 5.2).

Ritual design is buttressed by these fundamental principles: a ceremony must meet an identified need, take place in a specific context, with people who assume special roles; the content of the ceremony must make sense and be coherent with the couple's profile and values.

Need

The raison d'être of ritualizing is our profound human need. Most of the time this need is self-evident. Nonetheless, clarify it early on in the creative process. Declan and Nelia felt the need to ritualize their union and knew what they did not want. The civil ceremony they opted for did not mean much to either of them. Although this was the most obvious opportunity to consolidate their relationship with a vow, they can also use another occasion, such as their first anniversary, to introduce the heartfelt note they missed on their wedding day.

Context

Adequate understanding of context is crucial – effective ritualizing is influenced by the impedance of place and time. The variables of the broader context of a ceremony include getting time and timing as well as place and space to feel right.

Roles

Attributing the right roles to the right people requires an accurate grasp of the context. In the case of a wedding ceremony, the couple's relationship (♥) is at the centre of a ritual that they craft together. Friends and family participate actively and/or as witnesses of the couple's promise while a third person presides (see Figure 4.4).

Content

Elements such as meaningful words, gestures, music and objects constitute the content of a ceremony. This content unpacks and conveys to those present what is at the heart of the ritual. Meaningful ritual instils a sense of depth and significance for and among the group through visual and spoken messages. There is a felt sense that emotions are being contained or held by the context. This effects a felt shift as important concerns or uncertainty are dealt with through ritual. Meaning, containment and a sense of belonging to the group represent vital human emotional needs. Artistic elements in ceremonies contribute to the aims of the ritual and to support by the group.

Sensemaking

Making ritual that feels right involves *seeking, creating* and *taking* meaning (Holloway 2015). The couple *seek* meaning through their choices about the different aspects of the wedding ceremony such as venue, the content of ceremony, music, readings, dress, symbols and gestures, who participates and who is invited. They then use elements, in particular their promise, to *create* meaning. With their families and friends as witnesses, they *take* meaning from the ceremony, mark the transition and anchor it in their daily life.

Coherence

Coherence is the glue that holds the elements of the ritual together. There is consistency when (1) need and expectations are clear, (2) the roles are played by the right people, (3) in the right context, (4) expressed with suitable content, (5) that conveys meaning. Instead of investing in wedding rings they would not wear, two watchmakers sealed their vow with watches they made for each other. A couple working in a humanitarian organization chose to marry on a boat named for Henry Dunant (1828–1910), founder of the Red Cross.

RULES FOR RITUAL DESIGN

The craft of ritual design follows six design rules which keep the artisan on track during the creative process. Before Zumthor, the Bauhaus architect Mies van der Rohe said, 'No design is possible until the materials with which you design are completely understood' (cited in Borden 2010, p.7).[5] He encourages us to take into consideration their function and the broader context:

> We must remember that everything depends on how we use a material, not on the material itself… Each material is only what we make of it… And, just as we acquaint ourselves with materials, just as we must understand functions, so we must become familiar with the psychological and spiritual factors of our day. No cultural activity is possible

---

5   Mies van der Rohe's ideas were not new. Carlo Lodoli (1690–1761), an Italian architectural theorist and mathematician, anticipated modernist notions of functionalism and truth to materials. Mies's genius came from his ability to adapt these notions to the spirit of his time. His architectural forms and proportions were in harmony with the characteristics of the materials he used.

otherwise; for we are dependent on the spirit of our time. (Mies van der Rohe 1938, in Borden 2010, p.7)

Design rules also give a basis for evaluation of how well the design works. Steve Jobs is quoted as saying:

> Most people make the mistake of thinking design is what it looks like. People think it's this veneer – that the designers are handed this box and told, 'Make it look good!' That's not what we think design is. It's not just what it looks like and feels like. Design is how it works. (cited by Walker 2003, n.p.)

As a reminder of your role as the artisan of your ceremony, the first letter of each rule spells 'CRAFTS'. Once the two of you have gathered the elements that feel right, you are halfway to crafting your unique ceremony. Next comes the part where you put everything together to create a harmonious combination. These rules will help you craft rituals that work.

Create for our world

Time-honoured ritual elements – such as fire, water or salt – do not in and of themselves communicate meaning. The interpretation of such elements should be unambiguous. In one case, a young couple wordlessly introduced bread and wine into their non-religious wedding ceremony and left their guests with the task of making sense of the traditionally religious symbols in this context. In another case, a multicultural couple whose wedding theme was 'the spices in our life' served toast rounds spread with a mixture of spices from their respective countries to their guests at the end of the ceremony. The elements of the second ceremony fixed the couple firmly in their present reality, without neglecting their past. The rituals we create have the power to transform our future.

Respect for people and relationships

Harmonious ritualization respects people (present and absent), their relationships and interrelationships. The best-known summary of respect is the Golden Rule, which, in essence, means 'do no harm to oneself or others'. In the case of the confusing wedding ritual described above, a brief explanation might have made sense of the couple's use of traditional symbols – and put people at ease. Unlike animals, we communicate meaning with words and acts. When we choose to ritualize with keepsakes in the backs of our drawers, we should convey their meaning in a simple manner. Due regard for the feelings, wishes, rights and traditions of others strengthens social bonds.

Aesthetics serves need

'Aesthetics', a word derived from the Greek, refers to how we apprehend beauty through our senses, perception and feelings. Rituals are art-filled behaviours that transform everyday language, sounds and gestures. One couple hired a fashionable gospel singer to perform at their ceremony. About 3 minutes into her improvisation the couple showed signs of impatience; 2 minutes later they asked the celebrant to cut the singer off. The music was beautiful and well performed but, in this context, it was incongruous. It reflected neither the couple's taste in music nor the essence of their relationship.

Form follows function

'Form follows function', a main tenet of Bauhaus ideology, expresses the movement's reaction against design that hides the essence of an object under complex forms. In this context, the phrase is a reminder that the structure of the ceremony must fit the couple's ritual strategy. The heart of their relationship should be clearly stated. Any object introduced should be used during the ceremony. The ring bearer, for example, expects that the rings s/he bears will be ceremoniously placed on the newlyweds' hands.

Truth to materials

A carpenter uses a plumbline to true-up rough wood and works it until it is square, flat and smooth. Ritual craftspeople, like carpenters, must take time to true-up their materials. This begins with using the right person in the right place to say or do the right thing at the right time. The (true) case of the best man reading a declaration of love for the bride ('How do I love thee? Let me count the ways...') is an example of having the right person use the wrong pronoun. A couple who knowingly chose a wedding venue near an airport planned ahead for disruptions: whenever an aircraft flew over the garden the celebrant put the ceremony on 'pause' and the newlyweds serenely gazed into each other's eyes.

Simplicity: Less is more

Emotions tend to run high during a wedding ceremony. This reinforces the significance of the event but it also makes it hard for guests to concentrate. Complex concepts, sentences or ideas become difficult, if not impossible, to grasp. This is especially true for an outdoor ceremony where the number of distractions are compounded.

An elegant wedding ceremony is short and sweet. The Bauhaus-inspired brochure for Apple's first products proclaimed: 'Simplicity is the ultimate sophistication.'[6] The successful ritualmaker – whether beginner or advanced – uses a straightforward intuitive format, basic gestures and everyday unpretentious language. Communicate the heart of the ceremony (e.g. keywords) through repetition and short concise presentations in multiple art forms that appeal to the senses.

---

6   This quote is attributed to Leonardo da Vinci.

6

REALIZING THE
CEREMONY

On the day of the wedding Tyler, Joe and Joe's brothers arrive early at Battery Park. They suspend a red sari at the centre of the labyrinth and place a large container filled with sea glass on a stand. At the edge, near the benches, they set up a few camp stools and a simple sound system. As three Indian musicians and a French-Canadian fiddler tune their instruments, Joe slips off with his groomsmen.

Figure 6.1. Walking the labyrinth in Battery Park, New York City, NY, USA

© *J Gordon-Lennox*

Greeters welcome guests and guide them to the edge of the ceremonial space. When Tyler sees that the guests have gathered and that Amrita and her party are nearby, he takes his place in the labyrinth. At his signal, the fiddler begins to play and everyone stands.

ENTRANCE

'Golden Wedding Reel' by Louis Beaudoin, played by George (~3 minutes).

Wearing his grandfather's waistcoat and a new jacket, the groom arrives accompanied by his groomsmen and his daughter Sarah. When they reach the edge of the labyrinth, Joe pauses, shakes his groomsmen's hands and kisses his parents and daughter, then circles slowing to the centre where he takes his place next to Tyler.

Silence.

Instrumental version of 'Jashn-E-Bahaaraa' by A.R. Rahman, played by Ramesh, Kumar and Suresh (~4 minutes).

At the sound of Indian music, guests turn to watch the arrival of the bridal procession. First the musicians, then the bridesmaids in bright coloured long dresses enter the ceremonial space. The bride, accompanied by her father and mother, follow at a distance. Amrita's wedding gown is a long modern-style red robe; delicate henna designs decorate her hands and forearms. She lightly kisses her bridesmaids and embraces her parents. With her eyes on Joe, Amrita moves slowly through the labyrinth towards the centre.

WELCOME

Greetings to you all! My name is Tyler. On behalf of Amrita and Joe, I welcome you here today to celebrate their marriage. Some of you live in or near NYC, some of you have come quite a distance – from Washington state, Canada, India, the UK, France and Italy – to share this important moment in Joe and Amrita's life.

We have a special thought for those who are not with us today. In particular, we remember Amrita's maternal grandmother, and Joe's sister and his paternal grandfather.

You just saw Joe and then Amrita enter and walk to the centre of this labyrinth alone and meet in the centre. Unlike a maze, a labyrinth has no dead-ends; it encourages contemplation. Our fiancés walk the labyrinth today as a sign of their thoughtful decision to wed. At the end of this ceremony they will walk out of the labyrinth together as a married couple.

Since Amrita and Joe met five years ago, their relationship has been filled with joy but also buffeted by hard times. Much like the the sea glass glistening in this bowl, their love has matured and mellowed, giving it a fine patina. This wedding represents not a break but continuity in their relationship. They see marriage as a natural step in their life together.

You, the people they consider their closest family and friends, have been invited here to share this day as their guests and witnesses. As guests, it is your privilege to enjoy the lovely event they have planned for you. As witnesses, it is your responsibility to help them keep their wedding vow. So, please, listen carefully to their promise!

No one lives in a vacuum. Joe and Amrita need your support for the happy occasions, such as this, their wedding day, for the sad occasions that all of us must face, as well as for those simply ordinary days that many people find the most difficult of all. Do they have your support for the years to come? [Guests reply: 'Yes!']

READINGS

Live music accompanies the movements of the readers as they each step up with their texts. Halvar and Filippa describe how Amrita and Joe met and the importance for friendship for the couple. Nelia follows with the text the couple wrote about respect. Then Basie reads their take on the importance of generosity for a relationship.

DECLARATION OF LOVE

Amrita tells Joe of how, as a young girl, she dreamed of this day, how happy she is to be marrying him and to know that, together, they will face whatever the future brings. Joe describes one particular moment when he realized that he could not imagine life without her.

VOW

Tyler invites the couple to face each other. They stand hand in hand as he explains to the guests that the bride and groom will each pronounce their wedding vow in their respective mother tongue, then repeat it together in English.

Amrita / Joe

I pledge to continue to nourish and protect our love through respect, friendship, and generosity towards one another, those around us and the earth.

Exchange of rings

'Something Just Like This' by The Chainsmokers and Coldplay (~ 3 minutes).

Sarah presents the couple with their wedding rings. In turn they each give Sarah a kiss; she returns to stand with her grandparents. The couple exchanges their rings and kiss. Their guests cheer and applaud.

CLOSING AND EXIT
Tyler closes the ceremony saying:

'It is my honour to present Joe and Amrita, husband and wife!'

The bride and groom turn, look around the circle and smile at their guests. As the four musicians launch into a fast-paced piece of music, the newlyweds wind their way back through the labyrinth. As the couple step out of the ceremonial space they wave to their guests to follow them for brunch on the terrace of the SeaGlass Carousel. The wedding buffet menu is composed of Indian curries and poppadams as well as Canadian pancakes with maple syrup.

Figure 6.2. Sea glass

WHY WE RITUALIZE

We ritualize for many reasons, not the least of which is to feel safe and connected to others. Ritual feels meaningful and right when the vital concerns of a couple and their community turn ordinary language, gestures and movements into the extraordinary. Space and the pace of time changes – it may be slower or faster than normal time, bracketed off from the rest of life or on a stage of some kind. When rituals make sense, they provide us with a way to express what we care about and give us a safe container for strong feelings. Emotions are engaged in the most profound way. There may even be a sense that the ritual reaches out beyond the community and the universe to a time out of time where our humanity is shared (see Figure 3.2).

THE BIG DAY

During one of my first experiences as a wedding celebrant, I lost the flow of what was supposed to be a 15-minute outdoor ceremony where everyone was standing in a garden. The best man's endless stories about the groom and his ex-partners were followed by skits organized by the maid of honour and her children. As the impromptu presentations dragged on, the dignity of the moment evaporated and the newlyweds, their parents and the guests became impatient and finally embarrassed.

This ceremony did not go to plan. The right people contributed at the right time and place, but the materials were out of true with what the couple had intended as a solemn occasion.

In the preface to this book I observed that the success of a wedding and, perhaps, even the success of a marriage, can be measured by the authenticity of the wedding ceremony.

Although this couple's friends put us all in a difficult position, the ceremony 'worked'. The fiancés remained composed and decorous throughout. Time was suspended but we experienced the awkward moment, together, fully anchored in the present. When it finally came to the time for the couple to pronounce their vow, they did so sincerely and gracefully. At the cocktail, when they proposed a circle dance on the terrace, nearly everyone joined in with an exuberance that reflected their collective relief and solidarity.

Clearly, the fault for this faux pas lay with me. Although I could not interrupt the ceremony when it went off course, it was my responsibility to simplify and true-up these contributions during the two earlier phases (planning and creating). Last I heard, this couple was still together. Others are not so fortunate. One man recounts:

> My wedding was performed in Las Vegas by an Elvis impersonator in a gold jacket on a pirate ship. It was just the two of us. A real hoot. Six months later, on Valentine's Day, we filed for divorce in a drab but civil ritual. Next time around I'll go for something with a bit less fool's gold.

Whether or not the Las Vegas wedding was a spontaneous decision, the ceremony reflected how this couple saw their relationship. Their entertaining wedding ceremony was stamped with formalism, repetition, traditionalism – and consumerism. The soaring divorce rate is evidence of the blatant discrepancy between expectations for the wedding and for marriage. Ritual can be playful, but it is for real.

The values of the first couple described above are just as unmistakeable. In the end, it was their respect for the friends' well-meaning presentations that saved the wedding and served as a unifying factor that allowed their guests to acknowledge and support their commitment to each other.

Every wedding ceremony, wittingly or unwittingly, reveals how the newlyweds see their joint ritual profile, who is important to them and what they value most. 'Ritual has become one of the ways in which we structure and interpret our world' (Bell 2009 [1997], p.267). The ceremony reveals how couples deal with the world and its perceived forces and sources of power.

> **Three obstacles to a meaningful ceremony**
>
> The wedding ceremony feels right when the couple express mutual love – as well as their joy, loss and dreams – with their shared vocabulary and gestures. The greatest obstacles to a realizing a meaningful wedding ceremony are:
>
> - failure to keep the couple's relationship at the centre of the ceremony
> - a ceremony based on mistaken ritual identity and practice
> - ignoring one's gut feelings.

THE WORKINGS OF RITUAL

I have observed that the assembly's attention span is very short during a meaningful ceremony, be it religious or secular. People do not stay long with an emotion but spontaneously oscillate between tears and laughter, often in rapid succession. There are signs of physical release or discharge: a deep breath, moist eyes, yawning, a trembling in the face, lips or hands, or movements that stretch muscles in the shoulders, neck, hands or legs. As the ceremony draws to a close, people glance around, almost as though they are waking up, and then reorient themselves to the ceremonial space and the people around them. Tension leaves their faces and their movements become more fluid again.

When the ceremony flows in a gentle, harmonious manner, people say they feel supported. They may speak of a gut-level sense of joy, peace or completion. Fitting ritualization contains the emotions of the past in the past, and firmly anchors people physically and sensorily in the present, thus opening the way for transformation and new options in the future.

While my observations of these reactions are entirely subjective, sociological researchers Marie Bruvik Heinskou and Lasse Suonperä Liebst draw our attention to objective ways of measuring the feelings that unfold during social engagement in ritualization (Heinskou & Liebst 2016). They note that, in particular, Stephen Porges's landmark work adds new tools and methods to the scientist's toolbox.

REBOUND CAPACITY

Remarkably, trauma resolution and ritual that feels right both make use of our same innate capacity to rebound following an overwhelming experience. Biophysicist Peter A. Levine affirms that this capacity is biologically linked to an animal-like surrender to the sensate world within that is capable of awakening our life force (Levine 2010, p.256). Based on the observation that pain and pleasure cannot be felt simultaneously, Levine advises therapy that involves *titrating* strong feelings and *pendulating* between painful and pleasurable memories. The oscillation I observe during ceremonies is very similar. Although ritual may be therapeutic it is not therapy, and Levine has never applied to weddings the approach he prescribes for the resolution of trauma,[1] he does recognize that 'the tranquil feelings of aliveness and ecstatic self-transcendence that make us fully human can also be accessed through ritual. This way they become enduring features of our existence' (2005, p.xvii). More recently, Levine described ritual as 'an underestimated asset to healing trauma and restoring broken connections' (2017).

HARNESSING EMOTION

Ritualizing life events such as weddings can evoke different kinds of memories and feelings. Neurologist Robert Scaer's work on the therapeutic power of ritual in healing trauma shows that ritual practised in a group setting that feels both physically and emotionally safe is especially effective (Scaer 2006, p.53; 2012, p.143; 2017).[2] When intense emotions are

---

1   Peter A. Levine refers to this moving back and forth between emotions as pendulation, 'the primal rhythm expressed as movement from constriction to expansion – and back to constriction, but gradually opening to more and more expansion... The perception of pendulation guides the gradual contained release (discharge) of "trauma energies" leading to expansive body sensations and successful trauma resolution' (2010, p.80). He encourages 'titrating' emotion (keep it at a low level and go slowly). The acronym TRIPODS describes this process in healing trauma: Titrating, Resourcing, Integrating, Pendulating, Organizing, Discharging, Stabilizing.

2   Ritualizing in the context of a group in which we feel safe meets a psychobiological need for emotional attunement, because it engages 'the same limbic brain centres – the OFC, the anterior cingulate, and the insula – that inhibit and down-regulate the amygdala. With the amygdala inhibited, intrusive thoughts are banished and homeostasis is restored and healing is promoted' (Scaer 2012, p.143; 2017). 'The potency of ritual also may explain the impact of the eye movements of EMDR, the tapping procedures of EFT and TFT (Thought Field Therapy), and the repetitive affirmative statements of the latter two approaches' (Scaer 2006, p.53; 2017).

expressed and harnessed through ritual in a safe setting, they contribute to turning off what Scaer refers to as the 'fear generator' from the past. Ritual thus regularizes our perception of time and allows us to stay in the present to safely experience attuned relations with other people (Scaer 2012, pp.141–143). As authentic ritual grounds us in our senses, it can contribute to the prevention, healing and renegotiation of trauma. This process is reinforced by memory.

Figure 6.3. Sea Glass Carousel, Battery Park, New York City, NY, USA
©*The All-Nite Images CC-BY-SA*

The Book of Changes
A shock occurs, then there is a tremor caused by fear. This tremor is a good thing because it allows inner gladness and joy to follow. Even if rumbling thunder sows terror a hundred miles around, we remain so calm that we do not interrupt the ceremony by dropping the ritual spoon filled with spicy wine. (*I Ching,* Hexagram 51, circa 2000 BCE)

MAKING MEMORIES

Contrary to what was previously thought, memories are not permanent.[3] In the context of ritualizing this means that a ceremony that takes place in a safe setting is an opportunity to relegate painful sensations from the past to the past by updating a memory based on new information.

Rituals reflect our concept of time, how it passes and what that passing means. Recall during ritualization has the potential of switching off the fear generator and interrupting the somatic loops that involve negative repetitive thoughts, emotions, images or actions.

Upgraded sensations, in particular smell, form rescripted memories and emotions that, when accessed anew during ritual, empower rather than overpower.

RITUAL THAT WORKS

Each person present at a wedding ceremony experiences and takes meaning from it on different levels. At the most basic level a wedding ceremony 'works' when it fulfils three main conditions: promotes feelings of safety, reinforces the couple's sense of identity and commitment and keeps them and their community firmly anchored in the present. Some would add criteria that imply duration such as the partners' mutual satisfaction and the longevity of the relationship.

The ceremony is effective for the couple when they feel that they have indeed moved on from one phase to another and that the transition has truly been completed. It has the desired effect for newlyweds and their nearest and dearest when it inaugurates a new reality within which they can all evolve in peace.

---

3   Joseph E. Le Doux explains that the 'brain isn't interested in having a perfect set of memories about the past...instead, memory comes with a natural updating mechanism, which is how we make sure that the information taking up valuable space inside our head is still useful. This might make our memories less accurate, but it certainly makes them more relevant to the present and the future [i.e., adaptive]' (Le Doux quoted in Levine 2015, p.141).

SHARED HUMANITY

Anthropologist Barbara Myerhoff reminds us why we embark on this creative adventure:

> [Ritual] dwells in an invisible reality and gives this reality a vocabulary, props, costume, gesture, scenery. Ritual makes things separate, sets them apart from ordinary affairs and thoughts. Rituals need not be solemn, but they are formalized, stylized, extraordinary, and artificial. In the name of ritual, we can do anything. We can do astonishing acts. In the end, ritual gives us assurance about the unification of things. (cited in Broner 1999, p.37)

REALIZING PHASE

This is the final phase of crafting ritual. It involves preparation of the setting, opening, ritualizing and closing the ceremony, the social gathering and clean-up time.

A public wedding ceremony is intense and emotional, not simply because it transmits the meaning of the occasion from the couple to each one of their guests, but because it lets everyone present know what the other guests know. This lends a sense of cohesion to an often disparate group. The shared emotional experience – even if the ceremony consists of only a few words – launches an event.

On the day of the event, participants should arrive early and prepared. They should be welcomed by the presider who shows them where they will sit and stand, how to test and use the microphone and what cues they will receive to come forward for their presentation. Guests appreciate being greeted by people they recognize.

The presider is solely responsible for carrying the ceremony, holding the emotional container and respecting the time frame. The presider should stay 50 per cent with her/himself and 50 per cent with the couple and the assembly. This implies self-regulation while tracking other's sensations.

Keep the emotional container feeling safe by proceeding at an easy intentional pace. Use invitational language. Keep voice tone friendly and steady, and prosody pleasant.

In the event that emotions rise to an uncomfortable level, bring in elements of awareness (music, name the feelings you feel). Expand the experience through pacing and rhythm (this usually means slowing down). Broaden awareness of the body, restore sense of gravity, muscular tone, sense of time, orient to the presence of others...

Swiss celebrant Andrés Allemand Smaller specializes in multicultural wedding ceremonies. He believes that the guests at the wedding need to know at the outset why the couple called upon a professional secular celebrant.

> For many people, there is no such thing as a non-religious wedding rite, unless it is a civil wedding at the town hall. It is important that the guests understand that this ceremony is not an anti-religion statement. On this very special day, as the fiancés commit their lives to each other, they want to be completely truthful with themselves, each other and their guests. (2017, p.113)

Allemand Smaller also encourages the presider to tell the guests that they represent the couple's communities and that they intentionally brought them together for this occasion.

> In the past, their villages may have joined them in celebrating their marriage. Nowadays, those 'villages' have gone global; people come from around the world to be present. Yet, the meaning of the wedding has not changed. This is why I ask the audience to stand up when the couple walks in; with this simple gesture, what seems to be a disparate crowd suddenly starts identifying itself as the couple's community.

> During the ceremony, I invite the guests to witness the couple's commitment, but also to 'walk the couple into marriage', to help them *feel* what is actually happening. In this way, the guests support their friend or relative in the spirit of this unique wedding. In my experience, when the guests feel welcome and they sense that the wedding ceremony corresponds to the couple's expectations, they are happy to assume this role. (2017, p.114–115)

Ritualizing offers an opportunity to gradually and gently weave new meaning – no matter how bittersweet – into the fabric of our daily lives and inaugurate a new reality within which all of the participants feel they have moved on to a new phase in their lives and that they can evolve in peace.

RISK FACTORS FOR THE REALIZING PHASE

Costumed theme weddings, wedding ceremonies that borrow rituals and symbols from foreign traditions, religious ceremonies for the non-religious and vice versa are all to be avoided, because they inaccurately portray the couple's relationship and how they envisage their future together.

TOOLBOX

TOOLS FOR THE REALIZING PHASE

The toolbox contains basic tools for the realizing phase of crafting wedding rituals.

Guidelines for readers

As a reader you should ask if there will be a lectern on which to place your text and whether you are expected to project your voice or use a microphone. Arrive early at the venue to speak with the presider about your role, identify where you will sit and stand and test your voice. Ask the presider if water is available should you need it. You are responsible for having your text with you in a legible format. Avoid folding the text or storing it in a pocket. Make sure you are comfortable with your appearance and your voice is rested.

Instructions for text format

Print the text on one sheet of stiff paper (100–120g) that can easily be held with one hand. You may not have a lectern. Be prepared to hold a microphone with the other hand. Use only the top half of the page for your text. People tend to dip their chin down when reading the bottom of a page and this deforms the voice. Use a serif font (e.g. Times New Roman) in a large size (15–18) that is adapted to your vision and the conditions of the ceremony (sun/shade). Store the text in a transparent plastic folder; this is especially important when there is a chance of rain or drizzle.

Practise reading aloud

Read your text aloud at home three or four times. The Forbrain® device is an excellent tool for practising for public speaking.[4]

Test your voice in the ceremonial space well before guests arrive so that you feel at ease with the first words you speak. When using a handheld microphone, press it lightly against your chin and hold it there throughout the reading. The sound of your voice will be projected evenly, without being affected by the movements of your head.

Role and tips for the ceremony

Your role is very important, but, on this occasion, it is secondary to that of the newlyweds.

Walk up to the lectern at a natural pace. Exhale. Place your feet slightly apart. Do not lock your knees.

Standing rather than sitting during your presentation makes it easier to feel present and to be attentive to your audience.

If you feel nervous, lift your eyes, fix on a spot just beyond the heads of those in the last row.

Emotions may well up at some point. Let them. Exhale, then inhale slowly. Pause. Drink some water. You may want to comment on how this event touches you, or not. There is no need to make excuses for your interruption, just pick up reading where you left off.

Keep hand and facial gestures to a minimum. Link your hands behind your back or let them fall comfortably at your side; keep them out of your pockets. Do not to grip or lean over the lectern (it could tip over).

---

4   I use the Forbrain® device to practise reading aloud before a public presentation. After going through it three times I nearly have the text memorized (see Resources).

Ritualizing, step-by-step

The presider, much like an orchestra conductor, oversees all of the details of the event. From setup to the departure of the last guest from the ceremonial space, s/he stays in contact with the couple and liaises with all those involved in the ceremony.

Preparing the setting

Set up in situ for the wedding usually begins about 2 hours before the start of the ceremony. Depending on local customs and cultural expectations, this may mean guests arrive at the venue 1 hour before or 15 minutes after the time announced on the invitation. Whatever the expected time frame, the presider should arrive early. In addition to maintaining contact with the couple, s/he welcomes and briefs the 3 to 25 people directly concerned by the ceremony about their role and the timing: couple's parents, greeters, organizer from the venue, wedding planner, sound system crew, musicians, participants (readers), decorators, florists and caterers. Since photographers and video crews tend to arrive with the bride, contact them beforehand to ensure they remain outside the perimeter of the ceremonial space and do not block the view of family and friends in the first rows during the ceremony.

An hour before the guests are expected (there are always early arrivals…) everything should be ready and in place. At this point, the people active in the ceremony (presider, greeters, participants and musicians) are present and prepared. The sound system is in place, the musicians have set up and tested their instruments. Participants using a microphone have tested their voices (well before the arrival of the other guests). If the reception or cocktail area is within earshot of the ceremonial space, the caterers are now working quietly or getting ready to take a break for the duration of the ceremony. The minute the ceremony is over the caterers must be ready to serve food and drinks.

A reminder about the greeter's role

Since guests may be apprehensive about attending a non-traditional ceremony, it will be reassuring for them to be welcomed upon arrival by a person they recognize as a family member or one of the fiancés' friends. Greeters may be identifiable by a flower, a name tag or by programmes they distribute to guests.

Brief the greeters about where guests should leave gifts and coats, find the lavatory and water or juice, especially in warm weather. Give your greeters a copy of the guest list. Between them, they should be able to recognize nearly all of your guests and welcome them, if not by name, at least in a language the guest speaks. They may be asked to distribute programmes.

Upon a signal from the presider, greeters invite guests to the ceremonial space. Their role ends when the all the guests have arrived and the ceremony begins.

Opening and carrying the event

After consultation with the couple, the presider lets the greeters know that the ceremonial space is open to guests. The greeters may then welcome the guests and show them to their seats.

The presider takes his or her place in front of the guests just before the arrival of the couple. A change in the music – or a short silence if music is already being played – is an effective way to signal an entrance or a transition in the ceremony.

The presider is responsible for handling unexpected events such as late arrivals, crying children and noise from passing vehicles. Determine in advance who will intervene in the event of a medical emergency; this may be an organizer at the venue, a wedding planner or a greeter. The presider may need to modify the procedure, shift guests' attention or simply state what is happening; in most cases the ceremony continues as planned.

Transitioning from ceremony to social gathering

Preserve a dignified tone at the close of the ceremony. Since the couple usually exits first, followed by the parents and the wedding party, the presider should not have to interrupt the romantic mood with instructions about when and how to leave the ceremonial space. If there is a change of venue between the ceremony and the cocktail, an organizer or the greeters can ensure that guests move smoothly to where the social gathering is held.

Closing the event

At the end of the event, the organizer is attentive to people's needs as they make ready to leave, and s/he assumes responsibility for or supervises the clean-up.

NOTES ON THE ULTIMATE GUEST EXPERIENCE

The ultimate guest experience is enhanced by but does not depend on the venue, the food, the DJ or how much you spend. What matters is the encounter between people. How you organize your reception does influence whether people feel comfortable and enjoy the party. Most guests are honoured with attention from the newlyweds and they appreciate spending time with each other.

EATING PLEASURE

Give your guests something to talk about at the table. The farm-to-table movement has made healthy, earth-friendly foods more accessible than ever. Organic foods may cost more and travel from farther away but by using in-season, locally grown products you can keep the cost down and still guarantee freshness. Locally bought products that come directly from growers have fewer packing materials, spend less time in the fridge and require less fuel to transport it to you. One couple placed herb plants, like basil or cilantro in ordinary terracotta pots, on the tables so that their guests could choose which fresh herbs they wanted in their dishes.

Wedding cakes used to be good for photos or to eat but rarely both. Although you can now have nearly any flavour or colour you fancy, most couples still choose cakes in the multi-tiered format. Ask your baker if they would use locally sourced ingredients (like eggs and dairy products) in your cake.

DECORATIONS EMBELLISH

The adage 'simplicity is the ultimate sophistication' applies to decorations too. Ask yourself if the room or setting needs embellishment. If it does, how will any decorations you add enhance meaning or contact among your guests?

Joe and Amrita's favourite books placed at the centre of each table, along with a framed quote and a single flower, doubled as table themes and decorations. Even the shyest, most bookish guest could easily be drawn into conversation.

Look for party decorations that are the least toxic for the environment. One couple decorated the tables at their reception with a 'basket' they made out of painted shoe box covers that had been attached at two opposite corners. The following can be used as alternative decorations and activities:

- Tie ribbons onto sticks – for dancing around.

- Craft things – like origami – from old newspapers and magazine pages.

- Musical instruments can be made from recycled materials.

PARTY FAVOURS

Remember that 'favour' means an act of kindness beyond what is due or usual. Should you decide to offer favours, keep it them in line with the meaning of your wedding and your budget.

A couple who play rock music with a band of friends turned their wedding into a mock rock concert. Their wedding invitation was a VIP badge. At the cocktail and reception they had a fans' stand with a CD of their group's hits. Amrita and Joe handed out sea glass candy in cellophane packages as they moved among their guests at the cocktail. Another couple handed out pencils marked with their names and wedding date. Biodegradable seed packets will remind your guests of your big day long after it is over and are easy for out-of-town guests to slip in their suitcases.

ENTERTAINMENT

Eating and dancing are the most common wedding entertainment. Depending how you set it up these activities may, or may not, encourage people to meet and enjoy each other's company. Food trucks, tattoo booths, sky divers and casino tables may be all the rage but do they meet your criteria? Amrita had a table set up for her henna artist at the cocktail so that anyone who wished could have their hands done, or leave with a (fake) tattoo. What about story-telling? Folk and fairy tales from your heritage, recounted by your father or read by an aunt, can be a strong link to past generations. Stories about how you met or holidays with friends – illustrated with photos, objects or other visuals – also evoke a sense of place, culture and social history. The 'Paper Wedding' is a sweet story about a cross-cultural marriage (see Resources).

GUEST BOOK

Let your guests have the last word. The wedding day passes so quickly, and there is never enough time to spend the hour you'd need to catch up with that cousin or friend you so rarely see. Ask a young person to walk among the guests during the festivities with your guest book and a basket of inviting drawing and writing materials. One couple, who had their reception in a library, set their guest book – a recycled dictionary – on a table.

They asked their guests to choose a word from the dictionary, circle it, and then write them a note on that page using the word they'd chosen.

THE SECOND BOTTOMLINE

The exceptional organization at most good venues renders a wedding planner superfluous both for the ceremony and the reception. Pay attention to what is included in venue fees. Some provide tables, chairs, linens and audio equipment at no additional cost. Playing up the attractiveness of the venue with simple decorations you make yourself – such as your wedding vow wrapped with a bow instead of party favours – is cheaper, more inspiring and more original than paying for professional services and premium packages.

Have a friend or a relative liaise with the venue crew at the reception; not only can this be reassuring but it means you can enjoy your meal. In the role of MC this person may be a discreet behind-the-scenes presence to make sure not too much time elapses between the different courses, or out-front and entertaining. Either way their presence makes for warmer organization at less expense. In exchange, you can offer to assume the same role when they celebrate their wedding.

Other ways to cut down expenses include forgoing a live DJ for dancing. Perhaps you have a friend who loves to bartend, or you could ask the caterer to include several attractive non-alcoholic drinks and limit guests to one or two drinks instead of offering an open bar.

See other cost-cutting tips for the reception at the end of Chapter 4.

PART III

EPILOGUE

The wedding day is over. Do couples really get to live happily ever after? Part III addresses life in the years that follow commitment.

7

LIVING HAPPILY

The summer after Amrita and Joe's wedding, Tyler, the couple's presider, and his wife Kayla give birth to a son, Kylie. Shortly after that Aaliyah and Joshua announce that they have been blessed with twins.

Halvar and Filippa decide that for professional and family reasons they need to return to Sweden. When Thor was born in New York, Halvar got a half day off work and Filippa was given two weeks maternity leave. She quit her job as a doctor to become a full-time mom. At the birth of their daughter Zophia in Gothenburg, Sweden, both parents are entitled to a combined total of 16 months paid leave to care for the new baby and to integrate her into their family.

About the same time, Paul and Basie marry, in part to facilitate their adoption of four-year-old Kiarra, a child who was abandoned when she was diagnosed as being on the autism spectrum. A year later, Paul receives a good job offer in Paris, and the new family move to France with their dog Rusty. Basie sets up a B&B and becomes a stay-at-home dad.

After a few years of trying to conceive, Nelia and Declan opt for in vitro fertilization (IVF). The procedures are nerve-racking for both of them. From the first Nelia suffers from acute mood swings and weight gain. Although Declan wants to stop after the first attempt, Nelia insists on more trials. The physical and emotional strain, along with their mutual disappointment with not being able to bear children leads to their separation. Declan remarries a year after the divorce is finalized. Nelia leaves the group. After consulting her, Declan and his wife Olive join.

Fourteen months after their wedding, Amrita gives birth to their first child, Sumila. Two years later, their second, Jay, is born. They welcome each child with a tailor-made naming ceremony.[1] About the same time,

---

1   See Chapter 6 'Birth and Beginnings' and Chapter 10 'Death and Endings' in *Crafting Secular Ritual* (Gordon-Lennox 2017).

Joe's father dies of a heart attack. Six months later, Joe's daughter's mother takes a job overseas and Sarah joins the young family.

Joe and Amrita celebrate their fifth wedding anniversary with a trip to the zoo with the three children and their friends and their children. The occasion is made extra special by the presence of Halvar, Filippa, Thor and Zophia and Paul, Basie and Kiarra who flew in from Sweden and France. They all meet up at the monkey exhibit before spreading out on the grass in the park with a picnic lunch.

Later that afternoon, Declan and Olive arrive at Joe and Amrita's home to babysit and the couple leave for a more private celebration. In the warm light of the late summer evening, Amrita and Joe walk to the centre of the labyrinth in Battery Park. They re-read their wedding vow and recall the meanings they'd given their five keywords: protect, nourish, respect, friendship and generosity. They laugh at some memories and tear up at others. Things are so different from what they'd imagined! Three (!) children at home, Joe's father's death, Amrita giving up her job, moving house... Even so, they are amazed at the lucidity of their promise and how their keywords work like a shared code to structure their discussions and even influence the way they face joy and loss together. After a time, they slowly wind their way out of the labyrinth and stroll hand-in-hand to a nearby restaurant for an intimate candlelit dinner.

THE SEQUEL TO CINDERELLA

Did you ever notice that Cinderella – the classic model for love story scenarios – has no sequel? The plot ends with the dainty-footed young woman and her charming prince either driving off towards a sunset or living happily ever after, sometimes with lots of children. The storylines are suspicious, if not ominous, and sorely lack imagination. Nothing – certainly not youth or beauty – stays the same forever. And how many endings are truly happy?

The honeymoon phase literally draws to a close as the couple take up their daily routine. It is not unusual for one or both of the newlyweds to experience post-wedding blues. There can be a feeling of let down after any intensive effort. Major life events are particularly bittersweet as some things are gained and others lost.

It may be tempting to launch into a new project such as redecorating, moving or building a new home, changing jobs or having a baby. If you feel you need a challenge after the wedding, why not test your ability to fully enjoy free time, à deux? Amble hand-in-hand through a field. Stand still. Look about you. What do you see? Close your eyes and let the sun and the wind caress your face. Listen for birdsong. Sit for a time under a large tree. Feel the damp earth beneath you. What do you smell? Grasses, flowers or food smells wafting through the air? Share a few of those tasty cookies you finally had the time to bake.

Count six months to a year to absorb the effects of the new transition. In the meantime, if at all possible, put off taking on new projects that require further adjustment from one or both of you. Even if you and your spouse have lived together beforehand, from communication to finances to dealing with in-laws, marriage can be challenging in ways that courtship and cohabitation are not.

BECOMING AND BEING FAMILY

After touring the United States in the 1830s, Alexis de Tocqueville (2014 [1835], vol. I, ch. 10) commented on the state of women: 'In America the independence of woman is irrecoverably lost in the bonds of matrimony. If an unmarried woman is less constrained there than elsewhere, a wife is subjected to stricter obligations.' Nearly 200 years later, in the United States and elsewhere, most women and men aim for egalitarian coupleship.[2] Neither seem terribly interested in a Cinderella marriage where they must rescue someone from poverty. Daily duties such as cooking, cleaning and household repairs are no longer considered particularly gender-specific so there is relatively little difference in the division of labour among couples

---

2   A clear majority of people surveyed for a recent study of university students in Texas intend to marry or have a partner (approximately 85%), but only 51 per cent of the participants of rated both spouses working full-time/dividing childcare equally as 'likely' or 'very likely'. Even though the nature of marriage is changing, becoming more inclusive with fewer gender-specific roles, traditional assumptions about childcare predict the likelihood of women assuming primary childcare responsibilities for families with young children (Ogletree 2015, p.75).

who cohabitate, newlyweds and those without children. The valuable partner is one who can pull their own weight financially and conversationally.

Figure 7.1. The happy family, circa 1852
This full-page engraving was prepared by unknown women artists to illustrate a story by Alice B. Neal in a women's magazine known as *Godey's Lady's Book* (Godey 1852).
Clifton Waller Barrett Collection, University of Virginia

Emerging models of egalitarian coupleship (see Chapter 2) are echoed in the multitude of new ways of becoming and being egalitarian family units. These new family forms are influenced first of all by the acceptability of women bearing children later in life. Since 1970, the mean age of first-time mothers has gone up from 21 to 34 in 2016.[3] Second, being family now also includes couples having children outside of marriage. In 2014 in countries belonging to the Organisation for Economic Co-operation and Development (OECD) just under 40 per cent of births occurred outside of marriage (OECD Family Database 2014).[4] Third, couples may now become parents today through adoption, fostering, donor insemination, in vitro procedures and surrogacy. These changes look like progress and, in many ways, they are. Particularly for young women who are freer than ever to pursue further education and work towards professional goals and for couples who, for one reason or another, do not bear children.

PARENTHOOD: JOYS AND STRAIN

Ironically, even as the nature of marriage and being family evolves to become more egalitarian with fewer gender-specific roles, traditional assumptions about childcare predict the likelihood of one parent, usually the woman, still assuming childcare responsibilities when children are young (Ogletree 2015). As we saw, becoming a father had relatively little impact on either Tyler's, Joe's, Halvar's or Paul's professional goals. Kayla, Amrita, Filippa and Basie, on the other hand, stopped working – at least for a time – and then reduced their work time, or changed careers to accommodate their families' need for childcare.

The transition to parenthood highlights glaring contradictions

---

3   While first-time mothers in the United States were on the average 21 years old in 1970, the mean age of first birth rose to 26.3 years old in 2014 and only two years later the number of first-time mothers aged 30 to 34 surpassed that of new mothers in their 20s (Caplin-Bricker 2017; Cauterucci 2017).

4   Chile and Iceland are on one end of the scale of countries belonging to the OECD – an intergovernmental economic organisation with 35 member states – with birth rates to unwed parents at around or above two-thirds. Ten other countries (Belgium, Chile, Denmark, Iceland, Estonia, France, Mexico, Norway, Slovenia and Sweden) show a rate of over 50 per cent of children born outside of marriage. By contrast, five countries (Greece, Israel, Japan, Korea and Turkey) have rates of less than 10 per cent of children born outside of marriage (OECD Family Database 2014).

between the couple's egalitarian ideals and the suddenly inegalitarian conditions of their relationship (see Figure 7.2). New parents seeking therapy to help them deal with the radical changes imposed on their daily organization are often judged harshly. Any resulting marital conflict is all too often treated, even by professionals, as the couple's inability to adapt to new situations.

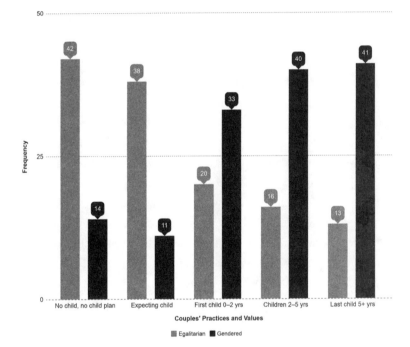

Figure 7.2. The effect of liberal welfare policy on family values and childcare
The division of labour among couples is increasingly shaped by welfare policies. This figure illustrates how childcare policies in liberal European states directly affect distribution of tasks within the family. While there is a clear tendency for couples without children to assume tasks in an egalitarian manner, this situation shifts radically with the arrival of the first child. Gendered division of labour then remains the norm, even after the children begin school.

Data source: Bühlmann, Elcheroth & Tettamanti 2010

ALL COUPLES ARE NOT EQUAL

Traditional theories of family behaviour struggle to explain the paradox of the couple's egalitarian values and inegalitarian practices. A study by

Swiss researchers on the division of labour among European couples (Bühlmann, Elcheroth & Tettamanti 2010) points to two significant factors that contribute to understanding this apparent contradiction. The first factor concerns the evolution of the individual's role in societies that are shifting from a strongly hierarchical organization to random neoliberal structures. While the former setting values stability and conformity to professional and family contexts, the neoliberal model favours mobility and requires people to constantly adapt and reinvent themselves. As young families with small children quickly discover, such adaptation definitely has its limits, particularly for couples with egalitarian values.[5]

A harder look at the broader socio-political context reveals a second significant factor for the contradiction between values and practice: welfare policies regarding childcare. In places with liberal systems, this tension is much greater than in socio-democratic regimes (Bühlmann, Elcheroth & Tettamanti 2010). In countries like the United States, Switzerland and Turkey where parental leave is not granted by law, the burden of childcare is placed on individual states and employers (Weller 2016). Countries with social-democratic welfare prioritize the wellbeing of new families – both heterosexual and LGBT – by often granting them a year or more of paid leave (see Figure 7.3). These 10 countries have the best parental leave policies in the world: Sweden, Denmark, Finland, Iceland, Serbia, Belgium, Norway, Hungary, Estonia, Lithuania (Weller 2016).

Halvar and Filippa lived in New York when Thor was born, so they had to adapt to the system there. Filippa gave up work to be able give their child the advantages he would have had in the socio-democratic system of their home country. Their second child, Zophia, was born upon their return to Sweden. Filippa had 18 weeks paid leave and Halvar 12 weeks off from work. The couple was also entitled to 480 days of leave, at 80 per cent of their normal pay, that they could choose how to split up between them.

---

5   The systems approach contributes significantly to understanding the changes in couple's interactions following the arrival of a child. Systemic theory of the family, also known as the Palo Alto School, grew out of Gregory Bateson's work in the 1950s. More recent influences include Paul Watzlawick, Salvador Minuchin, Mara Selvini Palazzoli, Fransisco Varela and neuropsychiatrist Mony Elkaïm.

Parental leave is not holiday time. Giving parents the means to dedicate themselves to caring for and bonding with their child reflects foresighted social values. According to trauma specialist Bessel van der Kolk, 'traumatized people are hurting for connection' (2016, n.p.). Early bonding and attachment enhance an individual's resiliency and their ability to connect with others. The Scandinavian model of childcare is one of the best investments a society can make in future generations. It serves as a hedge against trauma, and even delinquency.

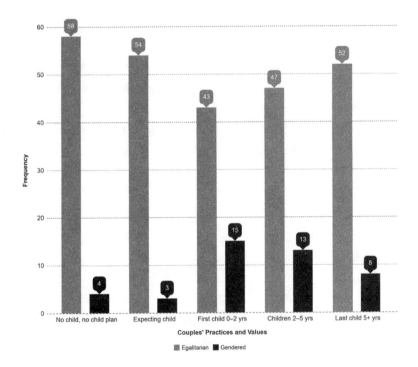

Figure 7.3. The effect of social-democratic welfare policy on family values and childcare
In stark contrast with the data from liberal states (Figure 7.2), the division of labour among couples living in European countries with social-democratic childcare policies barely changes with the arrival of children. Although there is a peak in the frequency of gendered tasks around the time the first child is born, egalitarian practice remains the norm. Furthermore, once children begin school there is relatively little difference in the practices of couples with and without children. The modus operandi for both groups is an egalitarian division of labour.

Data source: Bühlmann, Elcheroth & Tettamanti 2010

INVOLUNTARY CHILDLESSNESS

If having a child brings challenges, wanting and not being able to conceive one raises another set of difficult issues. In de Tocqueville's era, a woman's apparent infertility often meant repudiation of the marriage contract and abandonment. Accurate statistics about the success of in vitro fertilization are nearly as impossible to obtain as those concerning the number of couples that break up before, during or after fertility treatments.[6] Nelia advises couples who go in for fertility treatments to brace themselves for a physical and emotional rollercoaster ride:

> Declan and I had a great marriage, but the grief over negative results, early miscarriages and, even worse, the constant fear that it would never happen for us, because we were doing something wrong, eventually drove us apart. Each person fights to be a parent and experiences the loss of this dream differently. It was gruelling for both of us and certainly erased any vestiges of romanticism we might have had in our sex life. It destroyed my body; my health will never be the same. Looking to each other for comfort and support was not enough. Even if most of my friends with young children could understand my pain, I found being around them too hard to bear.

Many marriages do not survive the stress that accompanies the failure of IVF treatment – painful hormone injections, endless collection of sperm, loss of intimacy, a sense of inadequacy, frustration and shame, not to mention the anguish. And, as incomprehensible as it may seem, some couples split once the child finally arrives.

---

6   Danish researchers, who published their 12-year findings in *Acta Obstetricia et Gynecologica Scandinavica*, found that women who did not have a child were three times more likely to divorce or end things with their partner (Bachai 2014).

DIVORCE HAPPENS

The global divorce rate in 2017 was 44 per cent.[7] An estimated 40 to 50 per cent of all first marriages in the United States and 60 per cent of second marriages end in divorce (Warren 2018). The inability to conceive and related stressors are not the only, or even the main, reasons for divorce today.

SEX AND MONEY

In a dislocated world, where one cannot be too thin or too rich, what happens when partners lose their physical or financial attractiveness? Infidelity and finances top most couples' list of reasons for separation. These are followed by lack of communication, constant arguing, weight gain, unrealistic expectations, identity crises, lack of intimacy, lack of equality and not being prepared for marriage, as well as substance and physical abuse.

FREEDOM AND HAPPINESS

The end of a relationship, married or not, often coincides with a desire for freedom and happiness. In the individual pursuit of freedom and happiness, self-interest comes first. This can pave the way for either disinterest in commitment or lifelong adherence to a contract, however strange it may appear to others.

During a wave of anarchist violence in Europe (1892–1894) Italian immigrant Giovanni Rossi and his companions founded a colony known as Cecília in the state of Paraná in Brazil in 1890. Their anarchist utopian society advocated a collectivist way of life and economy without religion,

---

7   Unified Lawyers, a law firm in Australia, publish an infographic that illustrates divorce rates in countries around the world. At the top of the top ten list is Luxembourg with 87%, followed by Spain 65%, France 55%, Russia 51%, USA 46%, Germany 44%, United Kingdom and New Zealand 42%, Australia and Canada 38% (Unified Lawyers 2017). Countries with large Catholic populations, such as Chile, Colombia and Ireland, as well as Muslim countries like Libya, Uzbekistan and Bahrain often have lower divorce rates. The lowest rates, around 2–3% divorce, are found in two East Asian countries (Japan and Korea) and Turkey (OECD Family Database 2016b).

private property, family systems or hierarchical relations. In the end, it was free love that destroyed the Colony (Lapouge 2017, pp.52–55).

Freedom and happiness

Colony Cecília

...We will be free, we will be equal

Our idea will triumph. (Anonymous)

Forty years later, in another visionary venture, Jean-Paul Sartre (1905–1980) and Simone de Beauvoir (1908–1986) made a pact that committed them to the pursuit of freedom and individual happiness. They bound themselves to a life of infidelity and closed the exits of a conventional relationship. Their enigmatic 51-year-long intimate and intellectual partnership extends beyond the grave: Beauvoir is buried with Sartre at the Montparnasse Cemetery in Paris – wearing a ring from one of her lovers.

Today's consumer-driven world is littered with all sorts of contracts that we are not supposed to break. Yet, almost perversely, they also regularly tempt us to upgrade with a promise of even more freedom and happiness which ensure they remain forever illusive.

IN PURSUIT OF CONNECTION AND BELONGING

This guide begins with observations about the current shift in ceremonial ritual that untethers it from religion. Audaciously, it asserts that an authentic wedding ceremony is key to a successful marriage or partnership. The reader has now undoubtedly gathered that this is not a judgement of traditional religious or civil wedding ceremonies. Rather, it is an invitation to couples to reclaim ritual from institutional and consumer monopolies by crafting wedding rituals that correspond to their joint values and goals.

Our human need to ritualize life events like courtship, love and marriage is met when the rituals we practise reflect our notions of relationship and our dreams for the future. Rituals that feel right can support us as we marry or enter into unions and partnerships in an ever-changing world.

All wedding ceremonies are composed of three phases: planning, creating and realizing. Ready-made liturgical or civil ceremonies involve couples in the planning and realizing phases. The custom wedding ceremony requires time for the labor-intensive and often daunting creating phase.

At first glance, couples who require a totally personalized wedding ceremony – such as fiancés who do not share the same religious or cultural traditions and LGBT couples – appear disadvantaged. In fact, seizing this unique opportunity involves the fortunate couple in a threefold adventure during which they explore the foundations of their relationship together, create a meaningful ceremony that fits their commitment and give their entourage the ultimate guest experience.

ANCIENT PROBLEMS, MODERN SOLUTIONS

The sequel to the wedding day inevitably involves joy, but also sadness. Too many relationships finish in divorce courts; and all, eventually, end with death. Crafting meaningful ceremonies – be they for union or separation – is a profoundly human activity that involves the mind, the body and even the viscera. This age-old process of doing something to honour a life event takes the couple to the heart of their reality. Expectations for the relationship are expressed and revised. Connection and belonging are experienced and tested.

Practising rites that confirm bygone notions of an 'institution of marriage' is traditional only in the sense that it replicates the conclusions of tradition. The new ritual paradigm shift is about entering into the same problems as previous generations and crafting rituals that feel right today, rituals powerful enough to guide the couple through an uncertain future.

Perhaps, that is how tradition remains alive. And how humankind flourishes.

NOTES ON KEEPING YOUR RELATIONSHIP ON COURSE

We naturally invest time, money and attention in people and things we care about. When all goes well, it is not even necessary to check for signs that a relationship is on course. In times of uncertainty or conflict, however, if one or more of these points turn from positive to negative, the relationship needs extra attention. There's work to do. Relationships are living entities that need constant care and nourishment. In the early days after commitment you may feel safe in your relationship, more confident or at ease about being yourselves and less concerned about minor imperfections (yours and/or your partner's). Compromise takes precedence over being right.

As time goes on, you realize that you enjoy comfortable habits like sleeping on a certain side of the bed. Spontaneity may be out of the question because you are both really busy at work or you must plan ahead for a babysitter. You find that scheduled sex can be good too. And, if you don't put it on the calendar, that romantic evening out just doesn't happen. The way others see you changes too. While your parents may ask you less about your daily life (not that they don't care...), your friends may start coming to you for advice about their love relationships.

MUTUAL SATISFACTION

The relationship should meet the needs of both partners and, in the process, cause no harm to anyone – yourselves or others.

EXPECTATIONS

Over the course of time, people, their needs and situations change. In the early years of a relationship you may be inseparable and make love every day. Later on, you may need more time alone and less sex, or not. Tasks such as who takes out the garbage and plans holidays may shift from one to the other without affecting your love or respect for your partner. Revisit and take stock of your shared values, tasks and expectations regularly. These are all negotiable and renegotiable aspects of a relationship. Should either of you think something is worth discussing, then it is.

COMMON LANGUAGE AND CODES

Couples develop a private language, words or codes that facilitate communication in private and in public. A simple look from your partner across a crowded room can be all it takes for you to know that it is time to go home, or at least to move on to another venue. When it comes to disagreement this same acute awareness of your partner's feelings and needs may speak louder than actual words. This does not mean a good relationship is without arguments. Make it a rule to take a break whenever a discussion becomes heated. What hopes and fears does the situation raise? Find an alternative plan or answer that works for both of you.

JOINT PROJECTS AND PLANS

What projects and plans do you have going? Do you make a point of eating breakfast together every morning or share an evening cocktail at the end of each week? Some couples talk the entire time they are together, others enjoy companionable silence. Raising children, building or maintaining a home, supporting a charity, participating in sports are all activities that can consolidate a relationship.

LONGEVITY

Commitment is a long-term project. Staying together for the long haul does not necessarily mean occupying the same bed, or even the same home. 'Apartners' is a term used to describe the relationship of couples who share their lives but live apart.

Ultimately, the goal is not to do things together or even to be happy together but to *be* together. Life is fragile. Our days may be filled with happiness, but also with pain, sadness and anxiety. No couple is shielded against illness, accident, unemployment or ageing. Life changes and it changes us too. Authentic and meaningful living means accepting the full range of emotions. Aiming for contentment and joy rather than living happily ever after can feel more freeing – and take some of the pressure off.

WARNING SIGNS

Addiction to drugs, pornography, gambling, food or whatever, can be stronger than and even replace love for a partner. Anger is a normal emotion, but violence is never healthy. If one of you is addicted or tends towards violence seek professional help for both of you. In these situations separation and divorce may well be appropriate.

 # NOTES ON RENEWAL AND SEPARATION RITUALS

The recent vow renewal trend honours commitment as a work in progress. On the downside, it can give couples the impression that, like canned goods, their commitment has limited shelf-life, and that at some undetermined but critical point they must recycle or bin it. Beware of peer pressure to publicly renew your vows simply to demonstrate that the relationship is not dead or doomed.

Low-key intimate renewal rituals are at least as effective as a public re-creation of a wedding ceremony with 500 guests. The same goes for those that mourn separation. An untying-the-knot bash is likely to be of questionable taste. Ensure that whatever you do is not disrespectful of you, your former partner or the relationship you shared.

You have all the tools you need now to create rituals that renew your tie or mark the transition back to singlehood. Adapt the checklist and other tools in Part II of this book to craft the ceremony or ceremonial moment you need. The following examples show how rituals are rooted in the ability to pay attention to thoughts, feelings and bodily sensations, without judging them.

COMING HOME

After their return to Sweden, Halvar and Filippa felt as if they were floating between two worlds. Being with family and friends makes Filippa feel isolated. Halvar feels like he is out of sync with Swedish society. Recalling discussions with their New York friends about ritualizing even the small transitions in life, they realize that, in the busyness of the move, they have forgotten to set aside time to be alone together, and to resource themselves in nature.

Leaving Thor with his grandparents, they sail out on a weekend jaunt along the Swedish coast and drop anchor on an uninhabited island. Being careful not to harm any rocks, they build a fire and prepare their meal together. Both miss feeling like they have truly come home. After cleaning up, they strike out in opposite directions, looking for an object that symbolizes what they feel is missing in their return to Sweden. Halvar brings back four egg-shaped stones saying he wants to have a second child. Filippa's object is an abandoned bird's nest; she wants the family to move closer to her hospital. They discuss the pros and cons and then how to make it all happen. To seal their promise to work towards these goals they place the four stones in the nest take a photo to remind them of their plan. Now they feel ready to sail home.

BREAKING DOWN BARRIERS

When Aaliyah and Joshua approached Rabbi Leah about a renewal ceremony she replied with a question of her own: 'What's up? Has your marriage gone stale on you?' The couple laughed with her before explaining that, with the arrival of the twins, they'd begun treating each other mainly as co-parents. 'We want to do something symbolic to remind us we're a couple too.' The three came up with a plan: a month later, on their wedding anniversary, Joshua and Aaliyah leave the children with grandparents and return to the beach at Joshua's parents' summer home where they'd held their wedding ceremony. They spend some time listening to the roar of the waves and watching them roll in and out. They review the past year, then discuss their expectations and hopes for the future. Finally, Aaliyah, then Joshua, circle each other to symbolize their joint responsibility for honest communication, closeness and their renewed desire to break down any barriers that may come between them.

LAST SUPPER

After five years of marriage, Declan and Nelia admit that their intimate relationship has come to an end. Declan jokingly proposes they have a 'last supper' as husband and wife. The idea of a special dinner strikes home; neither wants to abandon their friendship. As Declan cooks, Nelia prepares two small boxes she calls their treasure chests. During the meal they celebrate the connection they enjoyed. To ritualize this process, and provide some containment, they take it in turns to speak and place in the other's chest a note, small object or picture that illustrates an experience or time they held dear. There was surprise and laughter as they acknowledge the strength of their bond. Over coffee, they talk about how they might move towards new ways of being together. At the end of the evening, as they each put the lid on their box, they remark how it feels right to separate now.

Both find it helps to have created these tangible reminders of their last supper.

CELEBRATING 20 YEARS OF COUPLESHIP

Shortly after moving to Paris with their daughter Kiarra, Basie and Paul prepare to celebrate their twentieth anniversary. Although the adoption ceremony brought them closer together and helped them define their roles as parents, their civil wedding ceremony had been a mere formality. They seize this opportunity to find a therapist to help them take stock of their relationship and renew their commitment to each other. They begin by identifying their joint values and choosing five keywords around which they compose a joint vow. Using tools such as *Prioritizing* and the *Coherence test* they plan a simple ceremony.

In the process, the therapist helps them see the extent to which Basie feels isolated in their new home. Paul's professional agenda is full, and his social contacts are facilitated by the fact that he speaks French. While Kiarra is picking up the language easily, Basie is struggling. 'It's not easy to strike up a conversation in a language I don't master. Especially as the only black guy in a playground filled with nannies, au pairs and mothers.' They decide to have a 'proper ceremony' surrounded by their old and new friends. This means postponing their celebration till summertime and looking for an appropriate venue. This is when they come up with the idea of setting up a B&B...

RENEW AND WELCOME A CHILD

Kayla and Tyler see devotion to their relationship as an essential element in their commitment to their newborn son. When Kylie is three months old, they ask Terry, their wedding celebrant, to help them craft a naming ceremony. Before the couple sets down their pledges to the child, Terry encourages them to omit the declarations of love from the wedding and concentrate on their tailor-made vow, adapting it slightly so that they can recite it together ('We promise to continue nourishing our love...').

During the ceremony Tyler recounts how when they married he and Kayla searched for, and found, a guideline that helps them keep their common good at the centre of their relationship:

> The advice of Rufus, a Roman Stoic philosopher, encourages couples to strive to outdo the other in devotion. We enjoy the challenge of competing with each other to see who is the more devoted spouse. When we realized that we were applying this same approach to being parents, trying to outdo each other to be the best parent for Kylie, we knew it could destroy our marriage and family harmony. As lovers who have become parents we now aim to be jointly selfless in a way that includes Kylie. If we are not able do that eventually Rufus's prediction will come true: we'll separate or remain together and suffer a fate that is worse than loneliness.

RESOURCES

CARBON IMPRINT
A multi-language website, www.myclimate.org, calculates the carbon imprint for different activities and modes of transport.

FORBRAIN®
Forbrain's dynamic filter trains the brain to be more attentive improving not only attention but auditory processing and sensory integration. Using the Forbrain device help people to improve speech fluency, pronunciation, sound discrimination and rhythm, for clearer and more effective communication. It also helps improve short-term memory, which impacts such skills as public reading and speaking. Available at www.forbrain.com

STORYTELLING
Fevered Mutterings. Accessed on 25 February 2019 at https://feveredmutterings.com/storytelling-resources

TED Talks with masters of storytelling and their new approaches to this age-old craft. Accessed on 25 February 2019 at https://www.ted.com/topics/storytelling

Walker, A.P. (1921) 'Paper Wedding' in *Sandman's Goodnight Stories*. Available at Project Gutenberg. Accessed on 11 March 2018 at www.gutenberg.org/files/20962/20962-h/20962-h.htm#chap20

REFERENCES

Adams, A. (2016) 'Divorce Rate in U.S. Drops to Nearly 40-Year Low.' *Time Magazine*, 17 November, 2016. Accessed on 7 September, 2017 at http://time.com/4575495/divorce-rate-nearly-40-year-low.

Allemand Smaller, A. (2017) 'Multicultural Wedding Ceremonies: A Journey into a World of Diversity.' In J. Gordon-Lennox (ed.) *Emerging Ritual in Secular Societies: A Transdisciplinary Conversation*. London: Jessica Kingsley Publishers.

Alexander, B.K. (2018) 'Bruce K. Alexander's Globalization of Addiction Website.' Accessed on 5 October, 2018 at www.brucekalexander.com.

Anderson, L.R. (2016) 'Divorce Rate in the U.S.' *Family Profiles* FP-16-21. Bowling Green, OH: National Centre for Family & Marriage Research. Accessed on 5 October, 2018 at www.bgsu.edu/ncfmr/resources/data/family-profiles/anderson-divorce-rate-us-geo-2015-fp-16-21.html.

Artigas, L. & Jarero, I. (1998) 'The Butterfly Hug Method for Bilateral Stimulation.' Accessed on 5 October, 2018 at http://emdrresearchfoundation.org/toolkit/butterfly-hug.pdf.

Asad, T. (1993) *Genealogies of Religion: Discipline and Reasons of Power in Christianity and Islam*. Baltimore, MD: Johns Hopkins University Press.

Aukeman, A. (2016) *Welcome to Painterland: Bruce Conner and the Rat Bastard Protective Association*. Oakland, CA: University of California Press.

Australian Bureau of Statistics (2016) 'Marriages and Divorces, Australia: 2015 Key Points.' Accessed on 5 October, 2018 at www.abs.gov.au/ausstats/abs@.nsf/mf/3310.0.

Australian Government, Attorney-General's Department (2017) 'Marriage.' Accessed on 5 October, 2018 at www.ag.gov.au/FamiliesAndMarriage/Marriage/Pages/Getting-married.aspx.

Bachai, S. (2014) 'IVF and Divorce: Couples Three Times More Likely to Break Up after Failed Fertility Treatment.' *Medical Daily*. Accessed on 5 October, 2018 at www.medicaldaily.com/ivf-and-divorce-couples-three-times-more-likely-break-after-failed-fertility-treatment-268184.

Bell, C. (2009 [1997]) *Ritual: Perspectives and Dimensions*. New York: Oxford University Press.

Borden, G.P. (2010) 'Preface.' In *Material Precedent: Typology of Modern Tectonics*. Hoboken, NJ: John Wiley & Sons.

Britt, R.R. (2006) 'Scientists Find First Known Human Ritual.' Science, 30 November, NBC News. Accessed on 5 October, 2018 at www.nbcnews.com/id/15970442/ns/technology_and_science-science/t/scientists-find-first-known-human-ritual/#.WqPJoRPwaL4.

Broner, E.M. (1999) *Bringing Home the Light: A Jewish Woman's Handbook of Rituals*. San Francisco: Council Oak Books.

Bühlmann, F., Elcheroth, G. & Tettamanti, M. (2010) 'The division of labour among European couples: The effects of life course and welfare policy on value–practice configurations.' *European Sociological Review 26*, 1, 49–66.

Caplin-Bricker, N. (2017) 'For the First Time Ever, Thirty-Something Women Are Having More Babies than Their Twenty-Something Counterparts'. XX Factor: What Women Really Think, 17 May. Accessed on 5 October, 2018 at www.slate.com/blogs/xx_factor/2017/05/17 cdc_data_says_women_in_their_thirties_are_having_more_babies_than_women.html.

Carter, C.S. & Porges S.W. (2013) 'The biochemistry of love: An oxytocin hypothesis.' Science & Society Series on Sex and Science (SSS). *European Molecular Biology Organisation (EMBO) Reports 14*, 1, 12–16.

Cauterucci, C. (2017) 'The U.S. Birth Rate Hit Another New Low, and Fewer Teens Are Having Babies'. XX Factor: What Women Really Think, 30 June. Accessed on 5 October, 2018 at www.slate.com/blogs/xx_factor/2017/06/30/fewer_teens_are_having_babies_so_the_u_s_birth_rate_hit_another_new_low.html.

Chang, S.T. (1986) *The Complete System of Self-Healing: Internal Exercises.* San Francisco: Tao Publishing.

Cohen, A. (ed.) (1991) *The San Francisco Oracle: The Psychedelic Newspaper of the Haight-Ashbury (1966–1968).* Berkeley, CA: Regent Press.

Cohn, D. (2011) 'Marriage Rate Declines and Marriage Age Rises.' Pew Research Centre. Accessed on 5 October, 2018 at www.pewsocialtrends.org/2011/12/14/marriage-rate-declines-and-marriage-age-rises.

Coontz, S. (2004) 'The world historical transformation of marriage.' *Journal of Marriage and Family 66*, 4, 974. Accessed on 5 October, 2018 at www.questia.com/read/1P3-725442551/the-world-historical-transformation-of-marriage.

Crawford, M.B (2015) *The World Beyond Your Head: On Becoming an Individual in an Age of Distraction.* New York: Farrar, Straus and Giroux.

de Tocqueville, A. (2014 [1835]) *Democracy in America*, vols I–IV, trans. Henry Reeve. Adelaide, Australia: University of Adelaide. Accessed on 5 October, 2018 at https:// ebooks. adelaide.edu.au/t/tocqueville/alexis/democracy/complete.html.

Dissanayake, E. (1992) *Homo Aestheticus: Where Art Comes From and Why.* New York: Free Press.

Dissanayake, E. (2009) 'Bodies Swayed to Music: The Temporal Arts as Integral to Ceremonial Ritual.' In S. Malloch and C. Trevarthen (eds) *Communicative Musicality.* Oxford: Oxford University Press.

Dissanayake, E. (2017 [2014]) 'Roots and route of the artification hypothesis.' *AVANT VIII*, 1, 15–32. Adapted from 'A bona fide ethological view of art: The artification hypothesis,' originally published in C. Sütterlin *et al.* (eds) *Art as Behaviour: An Ethological Approach to Visual and Verbal Art, Music and Architecture.* Hanse Studies vol. 10, Oldenburg, Germany: BIS Verlag Oldenburg.

Dissanayake, E. (2017) 'Ethology, interpersonal neurobiology, and play: Insights into the evolutionary origin of the arts.' *American Journal of Play 9*, 2, 143–168.

Donovan, J.W. (1891) *Don't marry; or, Advice as to how, when and who to marry* by Hildreth. New York: J.S. Ogilvie Publishing Company. Digitized version by Villanova University's Falvey Memorial Library. Accessed on 18 October, 2018 at https://digital.library.villanova.edu/ Item/vudl:466251#?c=&m=&s=&cv=69&z=-1.2662%2C-0.1271%2C3.2389%2C1.8018&xywh=-607%2C100%2C1881%2C775.

Fisher, H. (2016 [1992]) *Anatomy of Love: A Natural History of Mating, Marriage, and Why We Stray.* New York: W.W. Norton.

Gawande, A. (2011) *The Checklist Manifesto: How to Get Things Right.* New York: Picador Press.

Gendlin, E. (1962) *Experiencing and the Creation of Meaning.* New York: Free Press.

Godey, L.A. (1852) *Godey's Lady's Book 44*, January. Philadelphia: L.A. Godey. Illustration made available by Clifton Waller Barrett Collection, University of Virginia at: http://utc.iath.virginia.edu/sentimnt/gallgodyf.html, accessed on 20 March 2018.

Goldsen, J., Bryan, A.E.B., Kim, H-J., Muraco, A., Jen, S. & Fredriksen-Goldsen, K.I. (2017) 'Who says I do: The changing context of marriage and health and quality of life for LGBT older adults.' *Gerontologist 57*, S1, S50–S62. Accessed on 5 October, 2018 at https://academic.oup.com/gerontologist/article/57/suppl_1/S50/2904666.

Gontcharova, N. (2017) 'The Secret Reasons We're Spending More than Ever on Weddings.' 19 May. Accessed on 5 October, 2018 at www.refinery29.com/2017/05/155367/wedding-spending-survey.

Gordon-Lennox, J. (2017) *Crafting Secular Ritual: A Practical Guide.* London: Jessica Kingsley Publishers.

Gove, W.R., Hughes, M. & Style, C.B. (1983) 'Does marriage have positive effects on the psychological well-being of the individual?' *Journal of Health and Social Behaviour 24*, 122–131.

Grand, D. (2013) *Brainspotting: The Revolutionary New Therapy for Rapid and Effective Change.* Boulder, CO: True Sounds.

Grimes, R.L. (2014) *The Craft of Ritual Studies.* New York: Oxford University Press. The Appendices are on the Oxford Ritual Studies Series site. Accessed on 5 October, 2018 at http://oxrit.twohornedbull.ca/wp-content/uploads/2013/04/grimes-craft-appendixes.pdf.

Grimes, R.L. (2017) Front matter. In J. Gordon-Lennox, *Crafting Secular Ritual: A Practical Guide.* London: Jessica Kingsley Publishers.

Heinskou, M.B. and Liebst, L.S. (2016) 'On the elementary neural forms of micro-interactional rituals: Integrating autonomic nervous system functioning into interaction ritual theory.' *Sociological Forum 31*, 2, 354–376.

Herman, J. (2015 [1992]) *Trauma and Recovery: The Aftermath of Violence – From Domestic Abuse to Political Terror.* New York: Basic Books.

Holloway, M. (2015) 'Ritual and Meaning-Making in the Face of Contemporary Death.' Keynote lecture at Symposium: Emerging Rituals in a Transitioning Society, University of Humanistic Studies, Utrecht.

Holt-Lunstad, J., Smith, T.B. & Layton, J.B. (2010) 'Social relationships and mortality risk: A meta-analytic review.' *PLoS Med 7*, 7, e1000316.

Illich, I. (1973) *Tools for Conviviality.* New York: Harper & Row.

Immordino-Yang, M.H. (2016) *Emotions, Learning, and the Brain: Exploring the Educational Impulses of Affective Neuroscience.* New York: W.W. Norton.

Inaba, A., Thoits, P.A., Ueno, K., Gove, W.R., Evenson, R.J. & Sloan, M. (2005) 'Depression in the United States and Japan: Gender, marital status, and SES patterns.' *Social Science & Medicine 61*, 2280–2292.

Insel, T.R. & Carter, C.S. (1995) 'The monogamous brain.' *Natural History 104*, 12–14.

Jaffe, D.H., Manor, O., Eisenbach, Z. & Neumark, Y.D. (2007) 'The protective effect of marriage on mortality in a dynamic society.' *Annals of Epidemiology 17*, 540–547.

Jarus, O. (2014) 'Ancient Egyptian "Handbook of Ritual Power" describes love spells and exorcisms.' Live Science in Health & Science, *The Washington Post*, 24 November, 2014. Accessed on 5 October, 2018 at www.washingtonpost.com/national/health-science/ancient-egyptian-handbook-of-ritual-power-decribes-love-spells-and-exorcisms/2014/11/24/04a16ccc-70cf-11e4-ad12-3734c461eab6_story.html?utm_term=.8fa41bcdb60d.

Johnson, N.J., Backlund, E., Sorlie, P.D. & Loveless, C.A. (2000) 'Marital status and mortality: The national longitudinal mortality study.' *Annals of Epidemiology 10*, 224–238.

Jonte-Pace, D. (2009) 'Foreword.' In C. Bell, *Ritual Theory, Ritual Practice.* New York: Oxford University Press.

Knot (2016) 'Real Weddings Study.' *The Knot.* Accessed on 5 October, 2018 at www.theknot. com/content/average-wedding-cost-2016.

Kuhn, T. (1996 [1962]) *The Structure of Scientific Revolution.* Chicago: University of Chicago Press.

Lacombe, U. (2017) *Journey into Sound and into Oneself.* Varanasi, India: Luminous Books.

Lapouge, G. (2017) *Atlas des paradis perdus.* Paris: Éditions Arthaud.

Le Roux, D. (2018) 'Quand l'ours polaire s'habille des épines du cactus: les mutations que la préparation au mariage fait subir à la nature du rituel.' Intervention on 10 February at Sophiapol, Université de Paris Nanterre, France.

Levine, P.A. (2005) 'Foreword.' In M. Picucci, *Ritual as Resource: Energy for Vibrant Living.* Berkeley, CA: North Atlantic Books.

Levine, P.A. (2010) *In an Unspoken Voice.* Berkeley, CA: North Atlantic Books.

Levine, P.A. (2015) *Trauma and Memory: Brain and Body in a Search for the Living Past: A Practical Guide for Understanding and Working with Traumatic Memory.* Berkeley, CA: North Atlantic Books.

Levine, P.A. (2017) Front matter. In J. Gordon-Lennox (ed.) *Emerging Ritual in Secular Societies.* London: Jessica Kingsley Publishers.

Mandeville-Gamble, S. (2007) 'Guide to the Allen Ginsberg Papers.' Green Library, Department of Special Collections, Stanford University Libraries. Accessed on 5 October, 2018 at http:// oac.cdlib.org/findaid/ark:/13030/tf5c6004hb.

Medda, M., Serra, A. & Vigna, B. (1996) *Nathan Never* #59, 'Il torneo finale.' 1 April. Milan: Sergio Bonelli Editore.

Miller, G.F. (2001) *The Mating Mind: How Sexual Choice Shaped the Evolution of Human Nature.* New York: First Anchor Books.

OECD Family Database (2014) 'Share of Births Outside of Marriage.' Accessed on 5 October, 2018 at www.oecd.org/els/family/SF_2_4_Share_births_outside_marriage.pdf.

OECD Family Database (2016a) 'Cohabitation Rate and Prevalence of Other Forms of Partnership.' Accessed on 5 October, 2018 at www.oecd.org/els/family/SF_3-3-Cohabitation-forms- partnership.pdf.

OECD Family Database (2016b) 'Marriage and divorce rates.' Accessed on 5 October, 2018 at www.oecd.org/els/family/SF_3_1_Marriage_and_divorce_rates.pdf.

Ogletree, S.M. (2015) 'Gender role attitudes and expectations for marriage.' *Journal of Research on Women and Gender 5*, 71–82.

People's Path (1993) 'Lakota Declaration of War.' Accessed on 5 October, 2018 at www. thepeoplespaths.net/articles/warlakot.htm.

Perelli-Harris, B., Styrc, M., Addo, F., Hoherz, S., Lappegård, T., Sassler, S. & Evans, A. (2017) 'Comparing the benefits of cohabitation and marriage for health in mid-life: Is the relationship similar across countries?' *ESRC Centre for Population Change, Working Paper Series 84*, June.

Peterson, C. (2016) 'Ten Strange, Endearing and Alarming Animal Courtship Rituals.' The Nature Conservancy. Accessed on 5 October, 2018 at http://blog.nature.org/science/2016/02/09/ten-strange-endearing-and-alarming-mating-habits-of-the-animal-world.

Pew Research Centre (2015) 'Statistics of Unaffiliated Population by Region, 2010 and 2050.' Accessed on 5 October, 2018 at www.pewforum.org/2015/04/02/religiously-unaffiliated/pf_15-04-02_projectionstables82b.

Porges, S.W. (1998) 'Love: An emergent property of the mammalian autonomic nervous system.' *Psychoneuroendocrinology 23*, 8, 837–861.

Porges, S.W. (2011) *The Polyvagal Theory: Neurophysiologial Foundations of Emotions, Attachment, Communication, and Self-regulation.* New York: W.W. Norton.

Porges, S.W. (2012) Interview with William Stranger at Dharma Cafe. 6 June. Accessed on 5 October, 2018 at https://vimeo.com/44146020.

Porges, S.W. (2017) 'The Neurobiology of Feeling Safe.' In *The Pocket Guide to the Polyvagal Theory: The Transformative Power of Feeling Safe.* New York: W.W. Norton.

Sapolsky, R. (2004 [1994, 1998]) *Why Zebras Don't Get Ulcers.* New York: St Martin's Press.

Scaer, R.C. (2001) *The Body Bears the Burden.* Philadelphia: Haworth Medical Press.

Scaer, R.C. (2005) *The Trauma Spectrum: Hidden Wounds and Human Resiliency.* New York: W.W. Norton.

Scaer, R.C. (2006) 'The precarious present.' *Psychotherapy Networker 30*, 6, 49–53, 67.

Scaer, R.C. (2012) *8 Keys to Body–Brain Balance.* New York: W.W. Norton.

Scaer, R.C. (2017) 'The Neurophysiology of Ritual and Trauma: Cultural Implications.' In J. Gordon-Lennox (ed.) *Emerging Ritual in Secular Societies.* London: Jessica Kingsley Publishers.

Schirch, L. (2005) *Ritual and Symbol in Peacebuilding.* Bloomfield, CT: Kumarian Press.

Schnarch, D.M. (1997) *Passionate Marriage: Love, Sex, and Intimacy in Emotionally Committed Relationships.* New York: W.W. Norton.

Seligman, A.B., Weller, R.P., Puett, M. & Simon, B. (2008) *Ritual and Its Consequences: An Essay on the Limits of Sincerity.* New York: Oxford Press.

Tateo, L. (2016) 'Fear.' In V.P. Glaveanu, L. Tanggaard, C. Wegener (eds) *Creativity – A New Vocabulary.* London: Palgrave Macmillan.

Tateo, L. (2018) 'Affective semiosis and affective logic.' *New Ideas in Psychology 48*, 1–11.

Tomatis, A.A. (1988) *Les Troubles scolaires.* Paris: Ergo Press.

Troxel, W. & Holt-Lunstad, J. (2013) 'Marriage and Health.' In M. Gellman & J.R. Turner (eds) *Encyclopedia of Behavioral Medicine.* New York: Springer.

Unified Lawyers (2017) 'Infographic: Global Divorce Rates.' Accessed on 5 October, 2018 at https://5fg9x76nox-flywheel.netdna-ssl.com/wp-content/uploads/2017/11/love-of-divorce-rates-around-the-world.jpeg.

United States Census Bureau (2017) 'Household Income: 2016.' Accessed on 5 October, 2018 at https://census.gov/content/dam/Census/library/publications/2017/acs/acsbr16-02.pdf.

Urban Dictionary (2017) 'Coupleship.' Accessed on 5 October, 2018 at www.urbandictionary.com/define.php?term=coupleship.

Urban Dictionary (2018) 'Out-of-the-box.' Accessed on 5 October, 2018 at www.urbandictionary.com/define.php?term=out-of-the-box.

van der Kolk, B.A. (2011) 'Foreword.' In S.W. Porges, *The Polyvagal Theory: Neurophysiological Foundations of Emotions, Attachment, Communication and Self- Regulation.* New York: W.W. Norton.

van der Kolk, B.A. (2014) *The Body Keeps the Score: Brain, Mind, and Body in the Healing of Trauma.* New York: Viking Books.

van der Kolk, B.A. (2016) 'Fear – Gift or Curse?' Polarity's 8th Annual Zurich Traumadays, 24–26 June, Zurich, Switzerland.

Wade, L. (2012) 'Is Marriage a "Universal Human Value"?' Sociological Images, 3 October. *The Society Pages*. Accessed on 5 October, 2018 at https://thesocietypages.org/socimages/2012/10/03/is-marriage-a-universal-human-value.

Walker, R. (2003) 'The Guts of a New Machine.' *New York Times*, 30 November. Accessed on 5 October, 2018 at www.nytimes.com/2003/11/30/magazine/the-guts-of-a-new-machine.html.

Walker, R.S., Hill, K.R., Flinn, M.V. & Ellsworth, R.M. (2011) 'Evolutionary history of hunter-gatherer marriage practices.' *PLoS ONE 6*, 4, e19066.

Warren, S. (2018) '10 Most Common Reasons for Divorce.' Marriage.com. Accessed on 5 October, 2018 at www.marriage.com/advice/divorce/10-most-common-reasons-for-divorce.

Weddingbee (2010) 'Wedding Budget vs Salary Ratio.' Accessed on 5 October, 2018 at https://boards.weddingbee.com/topic/wedding-budget-vs-salary-ratio/page/2.

WeddingWire (2017) 'WeddingWire Celebrates 10 Year Anniversary, Highlighting the Evolution of Weddings.' Press release 17 May. Accessed on 5 October, 2018 at www.weddingwire.com/press-center/press-releases/2017/weddingwire-celebrates-10-year-anniversary-highlighting-the-evolution-of-weddings.html.

Weller, C. (2016) 'These 10 Countries Have the Best Parental Leave Policies in the World.' *Business Insider*, 22 August. Accessed on 5 October, 2018 at http://uk.businessinsider.com/countries-with-best-parental-leave-2016-8?r=US&IR=T/#sweden-3.

Winslow J.T., Hastings N., Carter C.S., Harbaugh C.R. & Insel T.R. (1993) 'Central vasopressin mediates pair bonding in the monogamous prairie vole.' *Nature 365*, 545–548.

Zumthor, P. (2006 [1998]) *Thinking Architecture*, 2nd edn. Berlin: Birkhäuser Architecture.

INDEX